An Indian Pilgrimage

An Indian Pilgrimage

Travel Notes of a Visit to the Indian Fields of the Church of Scotland

J. N. OGILVIE, D. D.

GYAN

Published by

Gyan Publishing House
5, Ansari Road
Daryaganj, New Delhi-110002
Phone: 011-47034999, 9811692060
E-mail: books@gyanbooks.com

Distribution Network
gyanbooks.com
India, USA, Canada, UK, Australia, France

ISBN: 978-81-212-9073-9 (PB)
First Published, 1922

2nd Impression 2023

Printed at: Gyan Press, Delhi.

An indian Pilgrimage
AUTHOR: J. N. OGILVIE

An Indian Pilgrimage

Travel Notes of a Visit
to the Indian Fields of
the Church of Scotland

BY

THE VERY REV. J. N. OGILVIE, D.D.

COMMISSIONER OF THE CHURCH OF SCOTLAND TO INDIA,
SEPT. 1921–MARCH 1922; CONVENER OF THE FOREIGN
MISSION COMMITTEE AND OF THE INDIAN
CHURCHES (CHAPLAINCIES) COMMITTEE

Printed for the Foreign Mission Committee of the Church of Scotland by

WILLIAM BLACKWOOD AND SONS: EDINBURGH, 1922

FOREWORD.

THE opening chapter explains sufficiently the origin of this book. Here it only needs to be said that, like the companion booklet, '*Afric's Sunny Fountains*,' which last year told of the writer's visit to the African Missions of the Church of Scotland, this, which deals with the visit to the Indian fields, is primarily a domestic document, written mainly for members of the Church of Scotland, on whose behalf the Pilgrimage was undertaken. It touches, however, on not a few points in which all the Churches are interested; and there has been a special pleasure in referring to several of the Missions of the United Free Church, whose Foreign Mission Committee honoured me with an invitation to visit their Missions too whenever possible. In another respect also the scope of the present publication is wider than that which dealt with Africa. Our Church's work in India is itself wider. We send chaplains to the Scoto-Indian as well as missionaries to the Indian; and both these activities are referred to here. There are 20 chaplains ministering to our own people, while 73 missionaries, men and women, and 383 Indian Christian workers, are engaged in the Missions of our Church. But in truth the work of all is one work wherever it is faithfully done, for the common object of the workers is to hold up Christ before the eyes of India, that men of the East and of the West alike may worship Him, and in Him find their true and lasting unity.

To the many friends who gave most willing co-operation in carrying through the long tour successfully, and in particular to the Rev. J. Drummond Gordon, B.D., B.Sc., Presidency Senior Chaplain, Bengal, for his invaluable help in planning every detail of the 9000-miles' journeyings in India, my fellow-pilgrim and I tender here our very grateful thanks.

J. N. O.

CONTENTS.

An Indian Pilgrimage.

CHAPTER I.

"MARCHING ORDERS."

THE "Marching Orders" for the Pilgrimage came from the General Assembly of the Church of Scotland, met at Edinburgh in the month of May 1921, and this, in effect, is how the orders ran:—

"Go, in our name, to India. Visit when there, so far as may be found possible, every Mission station of our Church, every Scottish congregation, and every Scottish regiment. Carry to our missionaries and our chaplains our affectionate greeting. Assure them of our unfailing confidence in them, our active co-operation with them, and our unceasing prayers to God on their behalf. Take counsel with them concerning the things that belong to the peace and prosperity of the fair city of God which they are helping to build in India; and bring back to us such knowledge of things as they are as shall enable us to do our part wisely and well as their fellow-labourers.

"And to the many Scottish men and women whom India holds, whether in the great cities or the isolated districts, whether engaged in commerce or in the service of the State, whether men of peace or men of war—to all alike give a message of warm regard from the old Church at home, in whose heart these sons and daughters of Scotland have a place from which they will never be dislodged."

Behind this stirring commission there lay two governing considerations. One was based on century-old memories, the other drew its motive force from the grave events in India to-day. It is one hundred years now since the period when the Church of Scotland began her work in India. In 1814 she sent there her first chaplain, the redoubtable Dr Bryce; in 1822 the Scottish Missionary Society, composed mainly of members of the Scottish Churches, gave to India its first Scottish missionary, the Rev. Donald Mitchell; and in 1830 the Church herself confessed her duty by despatching to India him who is still the most famous of all her missionary sons—Alexander Duff. Remembering these happenings of a hundred years ago, it was felt by the Assembly to be very fitting that the centenary of the Church's contact with India should not pass without some special recognition. But there was more than this behind the "Marching Orders." What might have been little more than a graceful tribute to the importance of long-past episodes was transformed into an urgent duty by the startling changes which are taking place in India to-day. It is a commonplace to say that *India is in transition*—but transition to what? None of all the men whom I have recently met in India—of the kind who think before they speak—have dared to answer that question with any definiteness. Hopes are abundant, expectations are plentiful, conditional prophecies are not few, but confident predictions are wanting. Still the transition process goes on, and scarce an institution or an activity in India is being left unaffected. Men who are in charge of agencies, great or small, which have India's welfare as their goal, are anxiously studying the signs of the times, that they may adapt their agencies the better to meet the changing needs. Christian Missions are markedly in this position, for "India in transition" means for them great and grave things alike in duty, policy, and destiny. So the General Assembly thought in 1921 when they appointed a commissioner to visit India, and gave him his marching orders.

That it was a commission not only to an important and anxious duty, but also to one of sustained strenuousness and difficulty, was manifest. But there were things that made it easy to discount the difficulties and to accept the call—the trust of the Assembly who gave the call, the anticipatory welcome already received from missionaries and chaplains in the field, the pleasant prospect of revisiting the land where twenty years of one's life had formerly been spent, and the hope of using the experience thus gained for the better performance of the present duty. Then, too, I was not to go alone, for to my wife the *Women's Association for Foreign Missions* gave a like authorisation to visit their Missions and their missionaries in India. So on 19th September 1921 *The Pilgrimage* began. A little company of friends bade us God-speed at Edinburgh station; another little company did the same at London, when we left for Tilbury Dock; and on 23rd September, in the P. & O. *China*, we sailed away towards India.

What we saw, and heard, and thought, and learned during the five months that followed is set down in these pages for the perusal of the Church in Scotland. The writing is frank and unstudied, informal and personal, as from friend to friend; and the hope that has inspired the writing is that the work of our Church in India may become better known, and better loved, and better served by all who read this narrative of an Indian Pilgrimage.

CHAPTER II.

THE FAR NORTH-WEST.

AFTER a voyage of three weeks, perfect alike as regards boat, weather, and company, on 15th October Bombay was reached, but for us at this stage the great western gateway of India was only an ocean junction. We were to enter by another door. From the big ship we transferred to a little ship, and in a few hours were literally leaping through and over the waters, hurled by powerful turbines at extreme speed, if also with some discomfort, towards our northern goal—KARACHI. Here on the morning of Monday, 17th October, we landed, and the long Indian trek began.

Geographically, Karachi lies nearer to Britain than does any other Indian city; yet so long as travel is done by rail or steamer, it will remain a city in a corner, less known to the average tourist than scores of less important places that lie on the regular line of march. All the same, it is worth knowing, for it is a great city, and if predictions of a golden future count for anything, its greatest days are yet to come. "Kurrachi!" ejaculates Sir Charles Napier in an eloquent outburst of affection, "you will yet be the glory of the East! Would that I could come alive again to see you, Kurrachi, in your grandeur!" If that famous old soldier did return he would see a city worth beholding—with noble harbourage, great warehouses, long ranges of imposing business blocks, and for miles around pleasant, even stately, homes of prosperous merchants—British, Parsee, and Indian. The outer environment, indeed, consists of an endless stretch of sandy desert and ragged scrub. But as a place to live in, those who are there are satisfied that Karachi is one of the best, and as the great port for the trade of the Panjab its lasting importance is secure.

No directly missionary work is carried on here by the Church of Scotland, but for more than half a century there has been a kirk and a chaplain ministering to the Scottish residents, and to any others who might feel an affinity for the Scottish service. We were to come across many such centres in our pilgrimage, and it may be well to state here once for all a few things concerning such Scottish chaplancies at civil stations. Indirectly but very truly they are essentially "missionary" in their influence, for their aim is to maintain in the Scot abroad the high principle and the religious outlook on men and things that are traditional in Scotland, and are a positive power for Christ in every land where they are found. For a Scottish chaplaincy in India to be entirely successful three things are more or less essential. There must be a seemly and, if possible, an attractive church, in which it is a pleasure for the average man to worship; there must be a chaplain who is a man's man, who can be in the world without being swallowed up by it, who has a message to preach, and who can preach it at least moderately well; and there must be a Scottish community sufficiently numerous to contain a nucleus of Scottish men and women, who are willing to feel and act towards the Kirk just as they did before they sailed away to India. Of the three, the central requisite is indispensable. Happily for Karachi, we found it in possession of all three. The kirk is an entirely worthy edifice, built sixty years ago by its devoted first chaplain, the Rev. William Middleton, who is commemorated in a good memorial window; and the chaplain, the Rev. J. Yule Rennie, and his people are mutually and with good cause well pleased with each other. Like every Indian congregation, it has had its ups and downs, corresponding generally with changes in the chaplain or in the personnel of the Scottish community, but the tendency to-day is upward; and the visit for the first time in its history of a messenger from the Church at home helped a little to lessen the sense of friendless isolation to which by its situation the kirk in Karachi is specially exposed. No service could have been heartier than that which was held on the Sunday evening, with a large congregation as glad to welcome the visitor as he was to give to them, first in all India, the warm message of affection from the Kirk at home. Lecturing, social gatherings, a congregational "At Home," happy private hospitalities, and many individual talks had filled the previous week, and on the Monday evening, with a grateful good-bye to our perfect host, Mr Gordon, a brother Aberdonian, and to Mr Rennie, we took train for Rawal Pindi, journeying *viâ* Lahore.

Of the twenty-four hours' run to Lahore there is little need to say much. It is over a monotonous level country of miserable scrub and sand. All the way through the Sind Desert it continued—fine impalpable sand, that drifted into the carriage all night long, so that in the morning everything, sleepers included, was white as with driven snow. But the journey was made memorable in another way. It gave us our first sensation of the 'atmosphere' of the "New India" we had come to see. Little by little as the weeks passed many elements of that atmosphere were revealed, some good and some —otherwise; but the initial awakening to the changes that had come occurred in the railway dining-car on the way to Lahore. We two sat at a small table on one side of the centre passage in the car, and on the other side were ranged four similar tables. The tables at the two ends were occupied by Indians, the two in the middle by Europeans, and through the whole dinner hour no talk at the European tables was possible for the boisterous shouting and laughter which passed between the occupants of the tables at each end. The car was theirs and theirs only—right of speech belonged to none but them! They talked and declaimed, while the European passengers ate their dinner in silence under this archway of flying vociferations. Truly this was a "New India" with a vengeance! One is glad to record that the episode remained unique of its kind throughout our Indian tour, but it made its contribution to the 'atmosphere.'

A further contribution was added at Lahore, where we spent a night and a day under the hospitable roof of Dr Lucas, head of the famous Forman College of the American Presbyterian Mission. Lahore itself was to be visited later, but a first glimpse was gained in passing of the "Young Christian India," which we were to see much of subsequently. The Annual Conference of this fine Mission had just been held, and had marked a new stage in the Mission's policy with regard to the relations between Indian Church and American Mission. Something approaching half-control over the Mission by the Church had been approved; and a keen young Indian Christian, in his early twenties, called to discuss the changes with the able missionary chief when I was present. The discussion was deeply interesting, but what impressed me most was the attitude of Young India in a discussion with one so much his senior in age, in experience, in achievement, and in sustained devotion. Absolute equality was implied throughout and most courteously conceded, but behind it was also an assumption of superiority in judgment such as few young men in the West would in similar circumstances care to parallel. Again, one gathered 'atmosphere.'

Another night's journey brought us to RAWAL PINDI,

the Aldershot of Northern India. A right pleasant sight it was after the sands of Sind and the bare country of sun-baked mud deposits, cut by the rains into weird crags and pinnacles, that mark the approach to Pindi. Pindi, with its splendid roads, attractive gardens, lines of welcome trees, endless bungalows, and spacious office buildings, to say nothing of its excellent hotels and, at this season, magnificent climate, was a delight. Specially gladdening was the sight of the beautiful Church of St Paul, permanent memorial of the fine work done here for many years by the Rev. George Roche, now at Brussels. No Indian chaplain in recent times has left so rich a legacy to the Scots of the future. It is a church of rare beauty, and neighboured as it is by an excellent manse, is a valuable possession of the Church of Scotland.

Unfortunately the chaplain, the Rev. G. C. Macpherson, who was returning from furlough, had required to extend his leave by a week, and to his regret and mine we just missed each other; but his faithful session were indefatigable in seeing things through. Sunday 30th October was the chief day. In the morning at West Ridge, three miles distant, the 1st Cameron Highlanders, who had only arrived the day before from 'summering' at Murree on the hills, paraded in full strength under Major Crichton, and I never wish to face a more reverent and attentive congregation. One felt the greatness of the opportunity that comes to those ministers whose work it is to keep such men in touch with the Eternal, and in contact, too, with their native land. Such work should be a joy and a strength to chaplain and to men alike.

In the evening a company of worshippers, not large, but very much attached, gathered in beautiful St Paul's, and together we sang the well-remembered songs of Zion, and strengthened one another in love and loyalty to the old Church beyond the seas. Here, too, one realised, as so often elsewhere in India, the far-flung line of Presbyterianism, and the bonds that knit us in unity. The prominent Mission here is that of the American United Presbyterian Church. Mr Heinrich, one of their staff, had officiated as chaplain during Mr Macpherson's absence, and by his great kindness I met one day the whole of his fellow-missionaries. Devoted servants of the Cross and true-blue Presbyterians, it was a pleasure to clasp hands with them and bid each other "God-speed" on our different paths of service. From Mr Heinrich's rich experience one learned not a little concerning the missionary progress in this wild northern land. It was good hearing. Difficult the strong men of the frontier are to win, but once won they stand fast. Here is an illustrative episode. A lambardar, the leading man in a frontier village, became a Christian, and straightway persecution began. His fellow-tribesmen burned his house and killed his wife, but they left himself untouched. He was a strong stalwart man of 6½ feet, so it was prudent to leave him alone. He held on, and by his grit and character and physical strength compelled respect, even though he was an aggressive defender of the faith. To the missionary he came one day and told his methods. "Not long ago, Padre Sahib," he said, "a man came and said bad shameful things about Jesus before a lot of my tribesmen. I could not bear it. So in my humble way I got up and took him by the shoulders. Then I ran him to a well, and held him right over it. 'Take back,' I said, 'all you have been saying about Jesus, or I'll drop you!' And, Padre Sahib, *he took it back, every word.*" Verily, they are strong men on the North-West Frontier.

Rawal Pindi marked our northern limit. On Monday, 31st October, we faced south and made for the PANJAB MISSION FIELD, very dear to the Church of Scotland by reason both of its history and its importance.

CHAPTER III.

THE PANJAB MISSION FIELD.

In the eyes of the Scottish Church it is holy ground which we now approach—sanctified by sacrifice and hallowed by victory. Our Church has five Mission Fields in India, and every field, as will be seen, has some special features that arrest attention and hold it fast. But the Panjab has more of these than any other. In historic interest the land of the North-West is an easy first in India, for this is the avenue along which in turn India's successive invaders have marched to victory, and the place-names of the Panjab are written in the history books of the whole civilised world. And her people's fame rivals that of their country. Britain's stoutest opponents they were until finally defeated, then Britain's stoutest friends in the hour of her greatest peril, and to-day the strongest of India's many races. In the future, as in the past, whatever plans for shaping India's destiny may be made by others of her sons, it may be safely said that the last word will lie with the men of the Panjab. To secure such a people means much for any cause, and in Indian missionary strategy nothing can take priority of the endeavour to secure betimes their allegiance for Christ. Their variety of race, too, adds to the value of their adherence, and intensifies the interest of the missionary enterprise. Mohammedan and Sikh, Hindu and outcast Chuhra, widely separated by religious creed and social usages—yet all are Panjabis; also, in varying degrees, men of grit and capacity, and, where work is to be done, men of action rather than of theories. Formerly foemen worthy of our steel, they are now brothers well worth winning. And that they are being won, visibly, rapidly, and increasingly, adds another distinctive feature to this field. The Churches of Southern India, where Christian Missions have been working for three hundred years, possess the vast majority of India's Christians; but next in order of numerical importance comes the Church in the Panjab, where Missions are little more than sixty years old. And so far as our own Scottish Church is concerned, the Christians of the Panjab easily hold the premier place. Connected with our five Indian fields are over 25,000 Christians; of these, 15,000 are found in the Panjab.

Ours is but one of a large brotherhood of Missions at work in this historic country, and the area definitely recognised and accepted as the Church of Scotland field is a strip long and wide that lies along the Chenab river, one of the five rivers of the Panjab. But it is 'some' strip. In the British Panjab Province, where the larger part of our operations are carried on, it embraces 4000 square miles with 2,000,000 inhabitants; and in two Native States on the north-east border, each 'occupied' by an outpost station, there is an additional area of 23,000 square miles and a population of nearly 1¼ million. Verily, a big responsibility this for the Church that has accepted it!

What is being done in the effort to discharge it? Eight leading centres have been garrisoned—Sialkot, Gujrat, Jalalpur, Wazirabad, Daska, Youngsonabad, Jammu, and Chamba,—fortresses held in the name of the Lord. True, one of these is at present without a European in the garrison, and in the others the garrison is weaker than it ought to be. But the posts are held, and the holy war is being waged; while from each centre numerous outposts have been established in the country round about. A great field and a great work; and here for three most memorable weeks we were now to be as busy as it was possible to be, seeing, hearing, learning, speaking, counselling and getting counsel, making new friends, tightening bonds with friends already made, and all through rejoicing in being, if only for a little while, active members of the Panjab Mission staff.

If I were to follow the order of our movements, Gujrat should come first, but a better grip of the Mission will be got by beginning at the centre station of all, SIALKOT.

CHAPTER IV.

SIALKOT—WHERE MARTYRS FELL.

IT was on a Saturday evening that we reached Sialkot railway station. Darkness had fallen, but when the train drew up at the platform, we looked out on such a gathering of missionary friends, all radiating welcomes by look and word and gesture, that Sialkot there and then became to us a city of light for all time coming, and gripped our hearts with a hold that nothing will ever loosen. Mr Scott, Mr Paterson, Mr Garrett, and Miss Plumb were all there, as well as numerous Indian friends-to-be; and Scottish Kirk and Panjab Mission for a little while did nothing but shake hands and shake again, and say how glad we were to do it. But yet better was in store. Mr Garrett's invaluable 'Ford' motor was waiting, and into it we got, along with Miss Plumb and Mr Garrett, and set off for the Ladies' Mission House, which lies two miles away. Soon the city was behind us, and we were out into the open country, driving along well-made roads. Crossing a bridge over a little stream, we slowed down. "Here is where the Hunters died," whispered Mr Garrett, and instinctively one's head was bared in reverent homage to the martyrs of 1857. But to this we shall come back. A little farther on we swung into a wide road leading to the Mission. In the darkness the houses were invisible, but quickly there was dazzling indication of their position. Rows of lights and graceful curves of brightness shone out high in the heavens. Coming nearer, they proved to be illuminations adorning the front balcony and roof of the Girls' Boarding School. Still nearer, and we approached the Mission House between rows of lighted standards, and passed under a splendid arch festooned with coloured decorations and inscribed with warm greetings. Then a halt. Rockets roared and screamed into the air, and dropped their starry rain. Slowly we neared the entrance, passing between two lines of Mission girls, each holding aloft a light with true Indian grace, their faces wreathed in smiles, and all singing with happy voices an ode of welcome. The heart filled with gladness and the eyes with tears of joy. Such was Sialkot's welcome to the messengers from Scotland's Church! And all the more touching did it become when we learned that every item had been planned and carried out by the girls themselves.

Had our arrival been by daylight the welcome would have been as cordial, but the witchery of night, the brilliant illuminations, and the excited joy of these daughters of India, who gave the welcome, added a fascination that will never fade from memory. And it need hardly be said that the welcome inside was equal in its fulness to that on the approach. Miss Plumb was an incarnation of joy and hospitality, worthy of Aberdeen; Miss M'Queen was hearty as a true daughter of Fife is bound to be. So it was that we came to Sialkot.

In the subsequent days the general plan of things became familiar. Nothing is cramped here. Spacious ground all around, with two good Mission Houses for the men, and one (in which we were happy guests) for the ladies. Connected with this latter by a covered way is a fine two-storey Boarding School and Dormitory, where over sixty Christian girls are housed and trained. In the adjacent compound stands the Hay Memorial Hospital—alas! at the time of our visit lying unused for want of a lady doctor. Trees and paths with well-kept floral borders surround the buildings, and make the settlement a home beautiful as well as a busy centre of Christian work. A little way off a shady avenue leads to the *Hunter Memorial Church*, and there on the day after our arrival Mr M'Cheyne Paterson guided me for the opening service of our Sialkot visit.

One's thoughts went back to that terrible day, 9th May 1857, when the Church's first missionary to the Panjab, young Thomas Hunter, his wife and infant child, were all slain by a mob of jail-birds who had been set free by the mutinous soldiery. Too late the devoted family had realised their danger. The whole district was in the hands of the mutineers, and the Hunters were driving for safety to Sialkot Fort, still in British hands, when they were overtaken on the road and summarily slain. Later the three bodies were found by the wayside, the little infant clasped tightly in the dead mother's arms. Thomas Hunter was one of the saints, even before he passed to the land where all the saints do from their labours rest. Only five months had he laboured at Sialkot when the call came, but in that time he sowed much fruitful seed. "The sowing," he himself had written a short time before he died, "may perhaps be all our work; *our* reaping-time in India may be already over, yet we know that you join in the confident trust that hereafter, in this place, there *shall* be a joyful reaping-time." He was a true prophet; and in the church that bears his name, I was to see the first of many evidences of his truth.

It is a goodly edifice the Hunter Memorial Church, built in the early 'sixties, and makes a worthy central shrine for the Mission's devotional life. The congregation that assembled was exceptionally interesting in its composition, though not at all typical of the ordinary congregations of the Mission—the sixty girls from the Boarding School robed in spotless white, and looking, as many of them truly were, a band of consecrated maidens; numerous sturdy crofters from the adjoining Christian village of Hunterpur, cultivators on the Mission land; several of the Murray College staff; the missionaries; and not a few other Indian Christians. Mr Paterson led the devotions. What I preached he re-preached in Panjabi, and the congregation were specially interested to learn that Thomas Hunter and my father had been class-fellows at Aberdeen University, and that when a boy I had often been told of the saintliness of the martyr of Sialkot.

An hour later Mr Scott took me to the second service for the day—parade service in St Columba's Church in the cantonment for Presbyterian troops in garrison. Over a hundred stalwart Ulster Presbyterians attended, men from the Inniskillings, and to them I had pleasure in giving a cordial greeting from their Church's Mother Church—the Scottish Kirk. One of the very many extras is this military work, which our missionaries have all along done gladly and right well. In the late afternoon came a third service, a simple Gospel meeting in a tiny church built by Mr Scott some years ago, away behind the cavalry lines, for the Christian servants connected with the cavalry regiments and messes—a little building, but neat and clean, and packed with 100 of a congregation, all devoutly attentive to the address, which was eloquently interpreted by Prof. Daulah, one of the Christian professors of the College. Not many mighty here, but just such a company of seeking souls as must have formed the early congregation in many a Gentile city in apostolic days. It was a memorable Sunday, eloquent of the varied ministries exercised by the Christian missionary.

Like all India the Panjab is a land of villages, and our Mission area is no exception. Numberless villages contain the vast majority of the people who are our care, and almost the entire community who now form the young Christian Church. In and around these villages the Evangelist, the Indian Pastor, and the elementary Teacher, as well as the visiting Missionary, are familiar figures. It is there that the visible successes of the Church most abound, and in extending and intensifying this 'country' work is the larger hope of the future.

But the Panjab has its cities too, and one of the most important of them all is Sialkot. Here, as in every Indian city where Missions are at work, *Education* of necessity forms the main activity of the missionaries. Time and again workers who have got impatient with the steady, unromantic, methodical methods of the school and college have diverged into lines that were more "direct" and that promised quicker returns for their labour; and they have often got what they deserved—up to a point. Then they have realised that to carry the Christian enterprise beyond that point, and give it a wide and a deep hold upon the people's life, the work of Christian education, from primary school to college class-room, cannot be let go. So it has been in Sialkot, where the throb of city life is felt, where the ambitions of Young India are strong, and boys and youths are ever growing into the men who have the shaping of their country's life increasingly in their hands. So let us to the Schools and to the College—the main Mission industries!

First the Schools. Mr Garrett, in whose able charge

Mission Council, Sialkot.

(*Left to Right*)

3rd Row—Mr Carter, Dr Hector, Miss Paterson, Mr Scott, Miss Stanfield, Mr Garrett, Miss M'Queen.

2nd Row—Miss Nelson, Mr Paterson, Mr Nicolson, Miss M'Minn, Mr Cook, Miss Rodger, Mr Alexander, Miss Stratton.

1st Row—Mr Dalgetty, Miss Kidley, Mrs Ogilvie, Dr Ogilvie, Miss Plumb, Mrs Alexander, Dr Hutchison, Miss Mackichan.

Professors, Murray College, Sialkot.

they are, is our delightful guide. They are two in number—a flourishing *Middle School* in the cantonment (the town that has grown up adjoining the old city, a consequence of the long British occupation), and an embarrassingly successful *High School* in the city itself. The 450 pupils of the cantonment School are assembled in the open space in front of the building when we arrive. A cordial welcome is given, and with brief Scripture reading and prayer the school is opened for the day. A short address from the visitor, and class after class in perfect order proceeds to its proper room. There we visit them in due succession, and see the boys at work. Right good work it is, and carried on under an Indian head-master and a goodly staff who know their business. Buildings are defective, and some of the classes meet in what can only by a stretch of courtesy be termed class-rooms; but the site is entirely good, and when the building scheme now approved (but delayed for want of funds) is carried out, all will be well.

Then on, in Mr Garrett's most welcome and indispensable chariot, to the *High School* in the city. It is quite a drive, for at least two miles intervene, but now the real "India" for the first time envelops one. The cantonment is behind us. The European is out of sight. Here everything is Indian—the brilliant colour; the jostling throngs; the strange mixture of rich and poor, of well-clad, ill-clad, and not clad at all; the babel of cries; the shouting of drivers as carts and ekkas and lordly motors of rich Indians get jumbled together in the narrow streets; the open shops that line the bazaars, with placid shopkeepers reclining at their ease, drawing bliss from their hookahs; the pungent odours and malodours that fill the air and titillate the nostrils. It is all "India" just as it used to be twenty years ago, the motor-car forming the one striking novelty. Underneath the sameness one knows that there are changes great and startling, but they do not obtrude, save that here and there in the flashing glance or contemptuous indifference of occasional by-passers whose look falls on us, one seems to discern a calm assurance that East is better far than West. In the very heart of the city is the *High School*, the nucleus of which—a house then worth £200—was gifted by an appreciative Government to the Mission so long ago as 1864. The School has grown mightily since then, and is now both overgrown and outgrown. Two junior departments have to be housed in neighbouring rented buildings, and the main building itself—despite successive additions and adaptations—is hopelessly cramped. Closed in as it is on all sides by other buildings, the very stones are crying out for an ampler site and accommodation worthy of the work. For it is fine work and no mistake. Nine hundred of the flower of Sialkot's youth—Mohammedans, Sikhs, Hindus, and a sprinkling of Christians—are here being daily trained for life, and along with the mental equipment that will fit them for their varied tasks a spiritual attitude is being fostered that cannot but tell for much good. A great charge is this of Mr Garrett's.

To the *High School* succeeds the *Murray College*. Here Mr Scott, the indefatigable, is our guide. With Mr Garrett and Mr Paterson for European colleagues, and a capable and loyal staff of eight Indian professors, three of whom are Christian graduates, several of the others sympathetic *Brahmos*, Mr Scott ably presides over a College whose importance can hardly be overestimated. Its students now total some two hundred, and there is no desire that the number should increase. In Christian Missions the method of small colleges, with a Christian staff, and the consequent possibility of the exercise of personal influence on a limited number of students, is to-day increasingly in favour. It is the aim of those in charge of the Murray College to pursue this method to its fullest possibilities. And if one may judge by the fine body of courteous and attentive young men to whom I spoke of some of the deeper things of life in the College Hall on the day of my visit, the possibilities are great indeed. The Murray College is the only College in the whole of the Sialkot district. From it have gone out in increasing numbers the professional men, teachers, lawyers, doctors, and employees in the various Government departments who are influencing their country and their fellow-men to-day. That such makers of the India of to-morrow should be trained in a Christian environment is from many points of view an incalculable gain.

'Murray'—why this name attached to the College? Because in the early days of the British occupation of the Panjab there lived in the new territory a fine Scottish soldier and Christian gentleman, Captain Murray, who admired and loved the Sikhs among whom he dwelt, and when he died bequeathed a sum of money, about £1000, to be used in planting a Christian Mission in the Panjab. From this came part of the means that made the College possible, and so the name—the Murray College. The College stands in a good position. Behind it runs a long row of hostel accommodation for students from a distance. Soon some greatly-needed extensions to the main building will be made, and a principal's house on land adjacent is in process of being built. So the good work grows from more to more, and in all the growth an appreciative Government lends a helping hand.

But what of the work for the *Girls of Sialkot?* Has our Mission no schools in the city for them? There is one such school—not large, but interesting. In the centre of the city up a narrow by-street, secluded as far as may be from the rude gaze of man, is a school for fifty Mohammedan girls—the care of Miss Plumb. Keenly interested in the visitors and happy at their simple lessons the little girls were on the day we visited them, and full of love for their devoted missionary friend, who is as welcome a visitor in their homes as she is a trusted and daily friend in the school. But the distinctive work for girls in Sialkot lies nearer home. It is that which is carried on in the *Christian Girls' Boarding School,* beside the Ladies' Mission House.

This is Miss Black's domain; and she, alas! was far off in Scotland on a much-needed furlough when we, her old friends, were in Sialkot. But Miss M'Queen was in her place, and the school was flourishing. One rejoiced to find so fine a building, both pleasing in appearance and entirely adequate in accommodation and arrangement. Sometimes in coming days we were to find neither the one nor the other, good work being done under some difficulties; but here everything was as it should be. The new Boarding House with its adjuncts is one of the best. Below, a good suite of airy class-rooms; above, spacious dormitories for the sixty happy maids who here are being "schooled." They are all Christian girls, drawn from the different stations of the Mission, the daughters mostly of Indian pastors or teachers or other Christians—girls who have shown qualities that here will be developed for the enrichment of the life of the Christian community in coming days. Round the classes we went, and it was a treat to be greeted everywhere by the smiling faces of the busy maids. In one room were the junior tots, forming their letters with shells upon trayfuls of sand; in another their older sisters were practising sewing, knitting, or other useful domestic accomplishments; in still others the inevitable themes of history, geography, reading, writing, arithmetic were being taught; and, of course, in every class religious knowledge had the prior place.

Hunter Memorial Church, Sialkot.

Girls' Boarding School, Sialkot.

Happy maidens these, and this the happiest time of all their life. No better work is done for the Christian Church in the Panjab than this. It is a "Ministers' Daughters' College" in a small way; but it is also a junior training-school for the future teachers and for the wives of the leading homes in the Christian community.

Other activities there are in Sialkot besides these, but on them one has not space to dwell. There is the *Hay Memorial Hospital*, a well-planned and well-built women's hospital that stands in the compound adjoining the Mission House. As already stated, it was "doctorless" when we were there, and the wards were tenantless; but with a doctor once more in charge there will be a welcome change. And there is the *Evangelistic Work* in the district round Sialkot, carried on at many villages, and diligently fostered by that prince of evangelists, Mr Paterson. Truly his time and strength are spent in many directions—as college professor, pastor-trainer, district superintendent, and general inspirer! To a mud-built village, JETHIKE, he took me one day, six miles out from Sialkot, and furnished an experience very different from the restrained orderly episodes of Sialkot life. In Jethike a Christian congregation flourishes under a vigorous catechist, Hakkim Shah. As his name betokens, he is a born ruler, a big bearded man who compels the respect of non-Christians as well as Christians. Before the humble church an open-air service is held, Christians grouped in front and a crowd of interested onlookers behind. Hakkim Shah leads the singing, which goes vigorously. The children grow restive, are rebuked—to none effect,—finally are summarily ejected by the masterful leader, while all the time the service proceeds. Rather distracting to a Western, but to an Eastern it is nothing. What counts is that there, in the sight of all the villagers, the God of the Christians has been worshipped; and a religion with notes of present gladness and future hope such as, apart from Christ, India knows nothing of, has been declared to needy souls. That more and more of the outside ring will be drawn to the inner circle is quite sure.

So it is that work goes on at Sialkot—and elsewhere throughout the field. The political unrest makes it more difficult than it used to be, and, as will presently be seen, it has some far-reaching effects on the Christian Church, but there is no halt nor stay with the soldiers of the King.

CHAPTER V.

GUJRAT—SITE OF BATTLE.

THE District of Gujrat holds some 760,000 of a population, mostly Mohammedans, dispersed among 1270 villages and 6 towns, the central town being GUJRAT, where our Mission was established in 1865 by the late Mr Paterson, first of a true missionary line. It was the earliest extension from Sialkot, from which it lies westward some forty miles by rail. Normally the missionary staff is five—two ladies working in schools and zenanas; two in the Dow Memorial Hospital, a doctor and a nurse; and one ordained missionary in general charge of the district.

It was on Monday afternoon, 31st October, we arrived, having come straight from Rawal Pindi, and this was really our first contact with the Mission Field. An imposing group of missionaries gave us glad greeting—the Rev. Mr Nicolson and seven ladies! Several ladies, fresh out from furlough, were there, waiting to be posted to their stations by the coming Council meeting. With the missionaries were a large number of Indian Christian friends, notably Mr Daniel, long the valued head-master of the High School, and Mr Mehtab Din, the local pastor. Mr Daniel had secured a motor from an obliging Indian friend, and after many introductions we drove off with Mr Nicolson to his hospitable home, some two miles away, which was to be our base for four very busy days.

Schools, *Hospital*, and *Church* are the Mission sights of Gujrat. To each a word before a further word on what at the present moment is most interesting of all that Gujrat has to show—the under-currents of conflict that are flowing in this ancient site of battle.

The *High School* is sufficiently well housed; and with its 450 pupils, schooled in 10 classes under efficient masters with a Christian head, amply justifies its existence. Some years ago there were 1300 boys here, but the uprising of other schools has caused a drop, which is not necessarily a misfortune. Quality rather than quantity is the true measure for Mission schools to-day, though a diminished fee income makes it less easy to carry on with the efficiency that is needed.

The *Girls' School* is of exceptional interest, but into it, in this conservative stronghold, no male foot dare enter. Happily my fellow-pilgrim's female foot was permitted, and accompanied by Miss MacKichan, Miss Kidley, and Miss Nelson, she visited the school, which lies in the heart of the town. Her welcome was a pleasant demonstration of regard for the home supporters of the school—garlands, songs, and an address in English read by one of the teachers, to all of which the visitor made suitable acknowledgment. One hundred and fifty girls here, radiant in the colours so dear to India. Mohammedan and Hindu, and a few Christians, they are all taught together, not one being a penny the worse, while all are a great deal the better for the wider fellowship. It was an innovation last year by Miss Mackintosh to combine two separate schools, and it has worked wonderfully.

The well-built *Hospital* and the stately *Church* are enrichments of the Mission, such as no other of our Panjab stations can boast of. Indeed, the *Dow Memorial Church* is probably the finest church in all our Indian Missions. Built by the Misses Dow of Montreal in memory of their uncle, and in keen appreciation of the value of the work carried on at the time by Mr M'Cheyne Paterson, the church is stately without, and—what is not so invariable in Indian churches—also all-beautiful within. Indian hands have carved the chaste communion-table, lectern, and pulpit; and at the "Welcome Service" held on the first afternoon of our visit, one rejoiced to see Canada's offering filled with a goodly congregation of India's people. In Gujrat and district the Christians number over 1200, and are increasing rapidly.

The *Hospital*, too, is a "*Dow Memorial*," built by the Misses Dow in memory of their mother. Here Dr Mabel Hector and Nursing-Sister Ellison Paterson, with a staff of four pleasant Indian assistant-nurses, were carrying on their priceless work of healing. The hospital is well placed on the edge of the city; but lately a Government hospital has been erected in its immediate neighbourhood, which makes the Mission hospital less indispensable for such women patients as shun all contact with Christianity. Yet the power of Christian kindness tells, and the wards are never without grateful inmates.

Gujrat is famous in history as the site where was fought the last decisive battle between the British and the Sikhs. It was a grim fight between two strong peoples, and touching it was to visit the little enclosure where lie the British dead, and do homage in thought to those young men—for most were quite young—who seventy years ago gave their lives for Britain's mastery and India's weal. So it is that the suggestion of battle will always hover around Gujrat; and to-day the place maintains its ancient character. Gujrat is one of the centres of the Indian irreconcilables. The Gandhi cap is frequent, and the Gandhi policy of non-co-operation has been very popular. A year ago, when this changeable leader had proclaimed the solemn duty of abstention of all scholars and students from Government-aided institutions, Gujrat hastened to obey. Our Girls' School dropped in a day from 300 pupils to a few stragglers. In the Boys' High School 100 boys withdrew from the 'polluted' class-rooms. Later this special line of 'patriotism' was abandoned, and the schools are very much as they were. But the spirit of antagonism to constituted authority and the fervour for 'Swadeshi' are more rife in this old 'Site of Battle' than in most places.

It is not a meaningless coincidence that in the Christian Church at Gujrat the 'Swadeshi' note was also found to be stronger than in most places visited. Politics are running riot in India to-day, and the Indian Church is inevitably affected. In the Church, as in the political world, two parties are found—the *moderates*, who seek to fit their Church for future independent life by a continuance of the present close co-operation with the Churches of the West; and the *extremists*, who, considering that the Indian Church is even now qualified to run alone, would hasten the dissolution of the time-honoured bond. In Gujrat one found not indeed this extremist policy, but just a little of the extremist spirit. Specially did this come to the surface when the vexed question of the right relation of the Mission to the fast-developing Indian Church was under discussion. In wellnigh every district in India where Missions have brought into being a living Church the question is debated to-day—and often with much warmth,—Has the Church advanced enough in knowledge and wisdom and sacrifice and restraint for the Indian Presbytery to become a partner with the Mission Council in the control of Mission policy and practice and finance? Most missionaries to the general question answer "Yes"; but there is considerable diversity of judgment as to the *extent* of the partnership. On this indeed it is impossible at the present time to lay down a fixed rule for all India, either as to the proportion of Indians who may well be given a place on a common Board, or as to the extent of such a Board's control over operations that are overwhelmingly dependent on home resources. The advance of the Indian Church in those qualities that make for full co-operation differs markedly in different areas. All that can well be said is, that with growing capacity ever greater co-operation will be gladly granted by a rejoicing Mission. Naturally there will be difficulty very frequently in agreeing as to the stage of growth that has been reached. That is inevitable. In Gujrat this difficulty is felt to-day, but one found that in frank and friendly talk the way to an agreement was not hard to reach.

. . . .

Ten miles from Gujrat, along a road which is one long avenue, is JALALPUR, famous in Scottish minds for one thing, Dr Lechmere Taylor's Hospital. Alas! Dr Taylor is no longer there: Edinburgh Medical Mission has claimed him. Nor is Dr Newton, his zealous colleague, there: God touched him and he went, some years ago. The hospital is still there with its 120 beds—empty! The needy patients are there, but there is none to receive them and give them healing. True, the Dispensary is there, and Subba Khan, the capable medical assistant, ministers to 100 out-patients every day. But oh,

Dow Memorial Hospital, Gujrat.

Dow Memorial Hospital Staff, Gujrat.

those 120 empty beds! Will no doctor come and put his hand to the work that was so splendid, and please God will be splendid once again?

The *School* goes on, and with its 250 pupils, almost entirely Mohammedan and Hindu, is doing capital work; and the charming little *Church*, built by Dr Taylor primarily for the hospital patients, is in constant use—an interesting experiment in architecture which seeks to give the Christian sanctuary an oriental touch. Mr Graeme Cook, who is in charge of the district, is entirely optimistic as to its possibilities, were it only adequately staffed. The villages number 183. Christians are found in eight of these; and for the whole of this field there is only one Indian catechist! It is a purely country district, in which the Christian folk number some 300. They gathered wonderfully in the little church on the day we visited the station—a very humble flock, but very grateful for any tending.

Another afternoon, SHADIWAL, five miles out from Gujrat, over a fearsome road, was visited. Truly an outcast people these were some twenty years ago—"the dirtiest and rowdiest in the Panjab." Then Miss Joss, a devoted missionary, went out to live amongst them. Plague came, and she fought it to the successful end. The people's hearts were won; and now a church, a school, and a *new* people occupy Shadiwal, right well served by two Indian ladies, Mrs and Miss Solomon. In the little church there gathered over 100 of a congregation, and the mass of eager faces, the hearty singing, the close attention, and the warmth of the greetings at the end are a splendid memory. It was a demonstration of the Gospel's amazing power, where any other power can profit nothing.

. . . .

One more Gujrat memory—a very delightful one, the best of its kind we have brought from India. In Gujrat the Deputy Commissioner, the big Government official, is an Indian Christian of high standing. His father is the revered Rajah Sir Harnam Singh, elder in the Scots Church at Simla, and one who for Christ's sake gave up his heirship to the throne of Kapurthala. His son, the Kunwar Sahib, as he is termed, was educated at Harrow and Oxford, and has for his wife the daughter of the late Dr Chatterjee, whose venerable figure at the World Missionary Conference in 1910 is well remembered. For culture and for power, alike of mind and spirit, this Indian gentleman and lady have very few equals. To meet them, as we did several times, in their own house at luncheon, one evening in the Ladies' Mission House, and again at a social afternoon of the Indian congregation, was a recurring delight. He a moderate Nationalist of the best type, and she a Christian lady of wide and warm Christian sympathies, they stand out in one's memory as Indian friends whom it was a joy to make, and an enrichment of one's life to keep. This, too, is 'atmosphere.'

CHAPTER VI.

WAZIRABAD—WHERE PASSIONS FLAMED.

IN 1919 passions flamed all over the Panjab, and threatened red ruin far and wide. Political animosities had been fanned by prolonged secret propaganda, and openly encouraged by a press that wrote wild things with strange impunity. Pernicious falsehoods concerning the actions and intentions of Britain towards peoples of the East of other blood and other faiths had been diligently circulated and credulously swallowed. Mr Gandhi's description of British rule as 'Satanic' was widely accepted as gospel-truth. Khiláfat agitators made the land ring with declamations as to Islam's wrongs and Turkey's shame; and in 1919 the inevitable result appeared, when the volcano belched forth fire and smoke and death. At Amritsar, only a few hours' run by train from Sialkot, Alec Stewart, manager of the branch of the National Bank of India, true son of the Kirk, good friend of my own, and one of the kindest and the best of men, most brotherly to every race, was beaten to death by the *lathis* of a maddened mob, and his poor body left to the flames. "Stand fast!" is the motto of his native Craigellachie, and he stood fast to the end. So it was with others also. '1857' seemed to be about to come again, when the second tragedy of Amritsar took place. To check the onrush of a maddened Indian mob, bent on murder and arson, General Dyer gave orders to his troops that brought death to several hundreds. Over this most grievous event much bitter controversy has since raged, in the course of which the first tragedy seems too often to be forgotten. Concerning *it*, there can be no controversy, but only condemnation of a crime black as any India can show. Of the second tragedy, defenders and accusers have both uttered sweeping judgments that are hard to justify. In this book of Pilgrimage one can only say, "Oh, the pity of it!" and leave the guilt to be apportioned rightly when calmer days give opportunity for calmer judgment. But that the tragedy averted, for the time at least, what might well have been a still greater tragedy, is confidently asserted by most of those who speak with personal knowledge of the district and the hour.

It was at WAZIRABAD that our Mission felt the flaming heat. An important railway junction this, and so in rapid touch with every wave of political excitement. The fury of Amritsar found a minor parallel in the madness of Wazirabad, and in the madness our Mission House was given to the flames. Two miles from the town along a country road it stood, quite defenceless should defence be needed. Dr Bailey, our missionary, got warning that a mob attack was likely, and just in time he and his sought safer quarters. That night his house and goods and many of his precious manuscripts were reduced to ashes ; and now only blackened walls remain to tell how, when passions flamed, the greatest linguist that our Church has ever given to the Panjab was rendered homeless. To-day the flame has died down. Quite dead ? Who shall say ? We at least saw nothing of it. But we did see much of a purer flame—a flame of God's own kindling, which has its source in love, not hate, and shines to cast light on life's pathway, and make man's journey thereon one of joy and brotherliness.

The Mission House is gone for the present, but the Mission abides, and under the diligent oversight of Mr Nicolson (from Gujrat, ten miles off) the good work proceeds, little the worse for what has happened. Three memories stand out of our visit to Wazirabad. First is the *Girls' School.* Here we were conducted by Miss Plumb, who came "ance errand" from Sialkot, thirty miles away, to guide us. Right in the heart of Wazirabad lies the school, and driving in a humble gharry from the station one was struck with the marked regularity of plan of this Eastern town—so unlike the twisted planless streets one usually meets. It has its explanation in the fact that the town-planner was Monsieur Avitabile, one of the four Frenchmen who rose high in the service of Maharajah Ranjit Singh, with whom we had so stiff a fight. Careers in India for European 'adventurers' were common in the old days ; and should certain things happen which some foretell, the breed would not be long in reappearing. But *false* prophets have not yet perished from off the earth. Meantime all thank Mons. Avitabile for a good straight road to our Girls' School. Some sixty girls are in attendance, gorgeous in apparel and radiant in colour. All are Hindus, and three Hindu widows do the teaching. The three are of long-standing and tried worth in the school, and for two years during the period of trouble, when Miss Plumb was not permitted to visit the place, they carried on the work unaided. Christian hymns were learned and sung, and the Lord's Prayer repeated daily—all the time that a Christian missionary was barred out by the anxious authorities. A Christian resident head is greatly needed but hard to find, for the town is not an easy residence for an unprotected Christian woman. Yet of the importance of this school in a Hindu citadel there can be no question.

The *Boys' High School* came next, and here Mr Nicolson led us. A fine building it is, just outside the city, convenient for access, with spacious ground for sports, and best of all, possessing a range of class-rooms that were a joy to see. The pupils number 450, and it chanced that on the day of our visit the Government Inspector was holding his inspection. It was over before our arrival, and in front of the school were gathered the whole of the pupils. Each class was by itself, and most picturesque they were, as, according to a pleasing custom on Inspection Day, every class wore turbans of a special hue. The effect was that of a beautiful garden of roses—groups of red and green and yellow and orange and blue, and other colours not yet attained by roses, all massed in orderly design. I asked the Inspector how things had gone. "Oh, excellently," was his answer. "This school, and your school at Daska, are two of the best in my whole district." Which same was very good to hear; and when I proceeded to address the boys I got 'good hearing' in another sense. A capable and sympathetic Hindu head-master controls the whole, while regular religious teaching is given in every class by Christian members of the staff, or of the Mission. The boys impressed one greatly. Intelligence and eagerness shone out from their faces, and marked courtesy and friendliness were everywhere. Garlanding of the visitors was generous, and the applause that greeted the bestowal betokened the happy spirit of the school.

Still one more episode—an unforgettable visit to NIZAMABAD, where a delightful glimpse of the "District work" was gained. Nizamabad is a large village, one and a half miles from Wazirabad, where a Christian congregation has been formed from the "depressed classes"; and week-day though it was, they had assembled, one hundred strong, to welcome the visitors, and hold a service of thanksgiving. To a sheltered nook we were led, where soon it is hoped a humble church will rise. Here the goodly company of men, women, and children were massed together as closely as they could pack—all outcasts, but redeemed by the power of Christ from their despised position, self-respecting intelligent folk of sturdy frame and simple faith. It was a great welcome. Padre Daniel led the service, and I addressed the gathering. Thereafter there was read a beautiful address of warm welcome, in which many pathetic words of gratitude for the work of the Mission were contained, as well as keen appreciation of the present visit. Then came an unlooked-for presentation—an Indian gold ring to my wife and a walking-stick to myself,—purchased with the willing offerings of a grateful community of those whom India calls 'untouchables'! We clasped hands with them again and again, and thanked God for the opportunity. When all was over the whole company convoyed us across the fields to where our gharry stood, and giving and receiving blessings, we journeyed on. A fine experience? Yes, and this is only one of scores of villages throughout the district where like congregations are to be found. Thanks be to God! His Kingdom cometh, and it cometh here with observation.

CHAPTER VII.

DASKA—WHERE PROPHETS GROW.

TWENTY years ago, had any one in Scotland, with an elementary knowledge of the Church's Missions, been asked what Daska was noted for, he would have answered unhesitatingly, *Prophets!* For there was the famous *School of the Prophets*—a modest 'Divinity Hall' planned by Dr Youngson for the training of men to minister to the masses of humble folk then crowding into the Church of Christ. Times have changed since then, and other methods of training are now in favour; but Daska may still be thought of as a place 'where prophets grow.'

It lies south-west from Sialkot, twelve miles by rail, eleven by road. Long identified with the name of Mr Scott, whose mark on the Mission will ever abide, Daska is now the charge of Mr Dalgetty; and when on a Saturday forenoon, in November, my fellow-pilgrim and I slipped out of the train at Sambrial, the nearest railway station, it was to be greeted by the heartiest of welcomes from the buirdly, genial, able missionary, whose kindly domination means much for Daska.

First came four miles over none-too-good road in Mr Dalgetty's own pony-trap, and then we transferred into a beautiful Hup mobile, very kindly lent by an Indian friend, in which we glided luxuriously towards our goal.

But after a few miles came a halt. We had arrived at Bhopalwalla, a large village peopled by Sikhs and Mussulmans, and quite a company of Christians. All members of the 'depressed classes,' these Christians, but now raised to *manhood* by the influence of Christian Missions, and eager to-day to give a rousing welcome to the visitors from far. So out from the car we got, and took our places in a great procession. In front was the 'band'—two bugles and two drums. Around and behind a great company of boys and men, several being Christian soldiers home from the war, and on the outskirts not a few women and girls. The band pealed forth a torrent of arresting sounds, and off we set along the dusty roadway to the village. Both sides were thronged by spectators of other creeds. Through narrow lanes and round many corners we marched, enveloped in dust - clouds wellnigh impenetrable. Fireworks banged continually, and though it was but midday, rockets were sent screaming into the air. Christian Bhopalwalla let itself go and enjoyed the process to the full; *and so did we!*

At last the little church appeared—too small that day for the congregation,—so in front we halted and sat down. Around was a circle of grave onlookers, Mohammedan and Hindu, and on the adjoining roof a bevy of Indian maids and matrons—all interested, and not ill-pleased that Bhopalwalla should do things well. Then a short service, when Mr Dalgetty interpreted my words of affectionate greeting, and one of the elders of the people responded. Telling of the gratitude of his people to Scotland for what had been done by the missionaries, he said they well knew how their friends in Scotland, in their eagerness to help the folk of Bhopalwalla, had not hesitated "to cut their own stomachs"! So he picturesquely described self-sacrifice. Whether truly or not, I leave Scotland to say. The service over, there followed much handshaking and kind speech. The procession re-formed. Dust and kindness once more enveloped us, rockets soared and shrieked, and amid cheers of cordial and touching friendliness we drove away.

A splendid introduction this to Daska, and it was grandly followed up. Daska was reached an hour later, and there, in the excellent Mission House, we were immediately at home. In front, beyond a little strip of ground, was the equally good Ladies' Mission House, where that evening Miss M'Minn and Miss Watt were our kind hostesses. And as the afternoon passed other welcomes came. First, headed by their fife band, appeared some fifty schoolboys, Christian boarders, happy and hearty as boys at home, and including in their musical répertoire not a few old Scottish tunes I used to play on the penny whistle fifty years ago. So I drew at once to these boys of Daska. Then a little later came a visit deeply gratifying. Twelve of the leading Indian officials, Mohammedan and Sikh, came to offer their courteous greetings. For an hour we sat and talked together of many things. Big, strong, friendly men they were, gentlemen all, whom in these days of difficulty it was a joy and a refreshing to meet. This visit was eloquent of the place our Mission holds in Daska, and of the respect which our missionary has won.

. . . .

At Daska we spent two memorable days, and as almost every hour was rich in experiences, I invite the readers of this Pilgrimage to give their company for these two days and see what we saw. For once the original diary notes are printed very much as they were written.

Sunday, 13th Nov.—A busy but most gratifying day.

10 A.M. Service in church, when fifty Christian boarders were present, and a great number of Christian villagers, men, women, and children. Padre James read the lessons, Mr Dalgetty took the service, Miss M'Minn was at the harmonium, and I preached. The whole service was most inspiring, specially impressive being the rich volume of song, familiar hymns and Indian Bhajans heartily sung to Indian tunes. Truly a miracle of God's grace and power to have raised in a few years these serfs to the status and consciousness of freedom in Christ. Strong men too they are, with faults like us all, but who will be a power for good in the land when Christ-controlled.

11 A.M. At the close of the service followed a dedication of reading-desk, pulpit, and communion-table—all of Indian workmanship, and waiting till now to be set apart to holy use.

11.30 A.M. A meeting in church with the elders, church workers, and representative members of the congregation. They read an address full of gratitude to the Church of Scotland, and affectionate appreciation of her missionaries. To this it was very pleasant to respond.

12 noon. Now came a unique service with the fifty Christian boarders. The *Christian Endeavour* movement is very active here, and these boarders are all in it—separated usually into a senior and a junior band, but to-day meeting together for the convenience of the visitor. The proceedings are strictly under the control of the chairman, a senior boy of sixteen. The subject for the day—the Parable of the Labourers—had been given out the previous week, and each boy had got an assignment. Called upon successively by the chairman, most give a three minutes' address (strictly timed) on the particular aspect that had been assigned them;

others read and others pray. The music is a great feature: two Indian drums, a hand harmonium, and fifty Indian voices! The boys sing with great power, specially haunting being the Psalms sung to Panjabi chants, finishing in quaint minor note, and strangely reminiscent of old Hebrew melodies. The speaking is a marvel, almost without exception excellent, and furnishing splendid preparation for future evangelists. At the end, with the permission of the chairman, I also had my three minutes.

Is this not something great? Where will you get anything like it in a boys' boarding-school at home? Yet you have it here in India, from boys who are mostly from the 'untouchables.' Good faces they have, rich in intelligence, and, as to-day shows, rich in capacity of speech and understanding. Truly, 'sons of the prophets' still grow in Daska, and the outlook is very bright.

4.30 P.M. Service in the church for the boys, and whoever else likes to come. It was taken by Mr Dalgetty, while I sat and saw and heard and pondered—not knowing the language, but discerning the presence and the power of the Spirit of God.

6.30 P.M. A delightful visit from Mr Das, the head-master of the Boys' High School, which we are to see to-morrow. He is a fine example of the best type of the young Indian Christian. Son of a Brahmin convert, he is a graduate of the Panjab University, and has character and capacity, as well as ideas and ideals, that make him a first-class head-master. Yet withal he has happily retained that quality of modesty, without any sacrifice of self-respect, which adds greatly to his efficiency. His wife, whom my fellow-pilgrim met at tea in the afternoon in the Ladies' Mission House, is equally delightful. A trained doctor and a lady of good birth, she is one of those cultured Christian ladies who are steadily increasing in number, to India's very great gain.

9.30 P.M. Retired to rest. Well earned, don't you think?

Monday, 14th Nov.—A day of further good things.

9 A.M. We were photographed with the young Christian Endeavourers. (Alas! the light was bad, and so was the photo; but later a photo of the Endeavourers alone was secured.)

9.30. The whole forenoon has been given to the High School, and has been an unqualified satisfaction. The school building is very fine. It encloses three sides of a large quadrangle. Verandahs run all round, and the class-rooms are abundant and airy. The work of the day opened by the whole 400 pupils assembling in the quadrangle for prayers. To the music of the drum-and-fife band the classes marched to their appointed places, and when all were seated on the ground the spectacle was beautifully picturesque, each class wearing a distinctive coloured turban, as at Wazirabad, and the same perfect orderliness prevailing. The Christian boys sang the opening hymn, Padre James read the scripture lesson, then, all upstanding, with one voice the Lord's Prayer was repeated by the whole school—a fine beginning to the day's work: and this is the opening to every day.

On the raised verandah where we stood were grouped Mr Das and his staff of masters. To each in turn we were introduced, and were most favourably impressed by their frank and loyal bearing; while Mr Das himself, quiet, capable, and self-reliant, was very evidently the right man in the right place. Then followed an address of welcome from the masters, a present of brass-ware, the product of the local industry, to Mrs Ogilvie, and an address of welcome from the boys. After suitable acknowledgment had been made, and the whole school

Christian Endeavour Society, Daska.

Physical Drill, Daska School.

addressed, the order rang out, the band struck up, and with some striking evolutions the boys marched off to the work of the day.

In the various classes, which I afterwards visited, the impression left was ever the same—the boys attentive, polite, diligent, the masters courteous and efficient, and the work excellent. From the school Mr Dalgetty led me to the maidan in front, and there in due succession the boys of every class took their turn of physical drill, given by a pensioned jemadar of the Indian Army. Truly an admirable school is that of Daska!

11 A.M. My lady readers may here leave and accompany my wife, under the guidance of Miss Watt, to visit the *Girls' Caste School* in the city, from which I was rigorously barred out. But it was clearly a sight well worth seeing. My wife returned from the visit charmed. "One of the best schools I have seen in India," was her verdict—and is still her verdict, when the tour is ended and scores of good schools have been seen. At the head is an extremely capable Indian Christian headmistress, Mabarak by name, the daughter of a Mohammedan convert from Sambrial. She is a teacher born as well as trained, and has her seventy pupils—Mohammedan, Sikh, and Hindu—all under perfect and happy discipline, and most efficient instruction. The religious element in the day's work is prominent. Christian hymns are sung, the Christian's Bible is read and expounded, while here, as in wellnigh every Mission school, the repetition of scripture passages is carefully encouraged. But perhaps the most striking evidence of the high intelligence of the pupils was given by their performing a simple play illustrative of life in the time of the old Moghuls. Action and atittude, words and gestures, were amazingly correct and lifelike, and improvised costumes of royal personages were worn by these maidens of the Panjab as if they were born to be queens.

Two languages have to be used in the school—Urdu and Gurmukhi,—the one for the Mohammedan girls and the other for the Sikhs. But the capable head, Mabarak, glides from the one to the other with perfect ease, and to one class presses home the instruction through this twofold medium.

2.30 P.M. Returned to the Mission House, packed, and got ready for the road once more.

And now, my friend, what do you think of Daska and our Mission there? I'll tell you what I think. It is one of the best bits of work in the Panjab—a bit that turns one into an optimist of high degree, and say, "Glory to God in the Highest!"

CHAPTER VIII.

JAMMU AND CHAMBA—WHERE RAJAHS RULE.

It is not a matter of indifference to Christian Missions in India whether the rule of the State is in the hands of the British Government or of Indian Rajahs. From the British they can count on benevolent neutrality and a fair field in which to work. Where rajahs rule they may get much more—or much less. It all depends upon the attitude of the rajah, or very often on that of the rajah's *entourage*. Hence it is that the personal charm of the missionary counts for so very much in Native States. Where he is liked, the Mission has royal approval; where the personal bond is less pronounced, the Mission is tolerated—but not favoured. Happily, in the two Native States on the Panjab frontier where our Mission works, Jammu and Chamba, the tie from the beginning has been singularly strong.

I. Jammu.

Jammu lies only some thirty miles north-east from Sialkot, but to pass to the one from the other is a physically refreshing experience. You come to a new land and a new people. The great plains, richly fertile but undoubtedly monotonous, give place to hills and mountains with land less fertile but vastly more picturesque; and for the towns of the plain, which are but a congeries of houses interesting only by reason of the people who occupy them, you are faced with mountain strongholds, that by their appearance transport you to mediæval days. Notably is this the impression made by the city of Jammu itself, high and lifted up above the river Tavi, with its turreted palaces and strong-walled fort, its 50,000 inhabitants clad in costumes of varying picturesqueness, and its famous temples, whose rich-carved spires shoot far aloft into the air. In the State of Jammu are 1,000,000 inhabitants, and over all rules as well as reigns His Highness the Maharajah of Jammu and Kashmir. Jammu is his winter seat, and is strongly Hindu; Kashmir, where the Maharajah betakes himself and 20,000 followers in the heat of summer, is as strongly Mohammedan. He himself is a devout and devoted Hindu, lavish in his gifts to Brahmins, and proud of the famous temples of his city.

Into this Hindu stronghold it was not easy to gain entrance. The first Indian evangelist of our Mission who tried it was summarily imprisoned and then expelled. But thirty years ago Dr Youngson, that truly great missionary and man of most persuasive love, won the Maharajah by his personality, and the Mission began. Every year added to the ruler's esteem of this 'man of God,' and conversations not a few on the deeper tenets of the Christian faith took place from time to time between the two. A school was established which has greatly prospered, a Mission House was built in which it is a joy to live, and among the humble Chuhra folk of the countryside the Gospel message got widely home. To-day the veteran founder is dead, but the work he began lives on, and under the devoted care of Mr and Mrs Alexander the cause of Christ grows steadily stronger. Not indeed with phenomenal rapidity—that is not to be looked for in a Hindu State like Jammu,—but little by little, step by step, the Church of Christ in Jammu moves onward. Over 600 there are now of a Christian community—200 in the city and 400 scattered through twenty villages in the district. The word of God has not returned unto Him void.

Two good days we had in Jammu, the fortunate guests of our *two* missionaries—for Mrs Alexander, formerly in charge of Sialkot Hospital, is as keen a missionary as is her husband. In these days we saw something of the forces that are against Christ as well as those that are working for Him. One morning Mr Alexander led me to the great Temple, and there one saw the power of Hinduism enthroned. Not one but many temples massed together in the centre of a vast enclosure. Round the walls of the enclosure run long ranges of chambers for the priests (poojaries) and their young acolytes. The temples are all alike, great basal squares, with dark recesses, where one discerns dimly the figures of many gods, and each basal block surmounted by a gold-covered spire gleaming in the sunlight. Connected with the temple and its worship is a whole army of poojaries, and fifty boys in training, all supported by the Maharajah. These we saw moving up and down, busy learning their mantras, but at the same time not unobservant of the visitors. One came forward to explain the glories.

Jammu Temples.

Scene on the Ravi River below Chamba.

"Thirty-three crores of gods," he proudly said, "are in the temple!" It may well be so, for one saw gods and godlings everywhere—the niches were crowded with them, and the very steps to some of the shrines were paved with scores of them. Vain imaginations all, but to uncover their vanity to those who now clasp them proudly to their hearts is a mighty enterprise of faith.

Of the forces on the other side, four memories stand clearly out. There is the *little school* we visited, up a narrow lane, in a quarter of the city where the Christian families congregate. Here some twenty boys and girls, children of the Christians, get their schooling. Quite humble folk they are, of the Chuhra class, but very keen that day, reading and reciting well, and answering Scripture questions very readily. From this material five boys have been recruited for the Christian Hostel at Daska, and six girls are in the Boarding House at Sialkot. In time they will return to be a power. Then there is the *big school*—a 'Middle Anglo-Vernacular' it is classified,—where 164 boys of Jammu, high-caste Hindus and Mohammedans, are getting a sound education from competent teachers under a sympathetic head, Mr Sanghi Mall, while daily is religious instruction given by Mr Alexander. Further, there is the *Christian congregation*, which met one evening in the little Christian school. No church building have we yet been permitted to erect, but here the Christians meet for worship. Over 100 were present that night, many of them municipal sweepers, who had only got free from their work an hour before. Two delegates were there from each of fifteen congregations in the district, some having come twenty miles to be present. The little place was packed, but none minded the packing. Brotherly enthusiasm was everywhere manifest. A short service and many addresses, presentation of two metal cups to the two visitors from Scotland, and speech after speech, in reply to mine of greeting, all telling of the keen appreciation of the Jammu Christians for the Mission, and their deep affection for the missionaries. A right warm-hearted people, full of love and loyalty—and possessing grit.

And last of all the sights that cheered was a small *Tea Party* at the Mission House! Four Indian ladies were present. One, a lady of Brahmin birth and high culture, head of the State Girls' School; another, the Inspectress of Girls' Schools throughout the State; the third, the doctor in charge of the Civil Hospital for Women; and the fourth, her assistant. *All four were Christians!* And this in a Hindu State where Hinduism is supreme! Yes, but Hinduism is not yet producing in sufficient numbers women qualified for such work as these are doing. Surely the mere presence of these Christian women serving their country in these important posts is eloquent of the place that Christianity is winning for itself in India's life.

Among the most-prized treasures of the great Jammu temple is a succession of ten large sculptures that fill ten darkened chambers round the base. They represent the ten incarnations of Vishnu. The Fish, the Tortoise, the Boar, the Lion, the Dwarf, Rama, Rama Chandra, Krishna, Buddha are all there—incarnations that are past. In the tenth chamber is the imposing figure of a White Horse. It is riderless, and is waiting for a Rider who is yet to come—the last and crowning incarnation, —waiting for One who is all holy, all good, all divine, sinless!

Is it not an unconscious cry for Christ and a prediction of His coming? Ay, even to Jammu? Only a few hundreds out of a whole million as yet own His Lordship and pray for His speedy coming. But though He tarrieth for a while, HE WILL COME!

II. Chamba.

Peerless for beauty among our Panjab Mission stations is Chamba, and unexcelled for loveliness by any spot in India. Yet, alas! it is the only one of all our Mission stations we had to leave unvisited. Reason why? Distance and time. It lies 100 miles to the east of Sialkot, and takes three days' travelling to get there. With three days' halt and three days to return, it meant nine days of our all-too-scanty time. So Chamba remains for us the *Dream Mission* of our Indian Pilgrimage.

It is not only in its scenic beauty that Chamba is supremely picturesque: its story as a Mission is unique among the Missions of our Church. It owes its origin not to the Church of Scotland, but to an enthusiastic minister of that Church—the Rev. William Ferguson, Chaplain to the old 71st Regiment, who, in 1863, being stationed in the Panjab, saw the great need for Christian Missions, resigned his chaplaincy, and offered himself to the Church of Scotland as its first missionary to Chamba. Alas! there were no funds for this fresh venture, and the Church said 'No.' But Ferguson heeded not. With his like-minded wife he went to Chamba, won the Rajah's heart, and there and then began a Mission, trusting that God would see him through. The story of those early years reads like a romance, for the missionary's ways were most romantic. Robed in gown and bands, he perambulated the city day after day after his first arrival, accompanied by two Indian assistants, and proclaimed, first in English, then in Hindi, then in Hindustani, the 'Good News' through some striking text. The texts changed from day to day, but the message was the same. The Rajah was impressed, came out from the palace, and made salaam to this strange messenger of God, and offered a donation to maintain the missionary for a year! The gates of Chamba were opened, and the missionary entered in.

By methods of like impressiveness, and with apostolic zeal, the missionary toiled for some ten years, when the ill-health of Mrs Ferguson compelled him to give up. The Church of that day, appreciating the fine spirit of the worker and the good work done, took over the Mission, and added it to the Panjab Mission Field. The Mission was flourishing and hopeful—two congregations, a community of 160 Christians, a school for Christian children, classes for Christian men and women, 22 Zenanas open to Mrs Ferguson, including the palace, and a Girls' school commenced. And all this in the heart of a country where every prospect pleases.

Let Dr Youngson tell its beauties :—

"The traveller from the plains, as he ascends hill after hill till he reaches the ridge of the mountain on which Dalhousie lies, walks successively through groves of flowering shrubs and forests of pine, rhododendron, and oak, the rich green carpet beneath having woven into it at different elevations different flowers—lilies, forget-me-nots, strawberry blossom, primroses, daisies, violets, and many more; while climbing roses in a profusion of red and white blossoms light up the dark-green of the trees.

"Still higher among the lofty pines he goes, until, gradually descending into the valley of the Ravi, he passes under the shadow of dark cedars clustering about the pool of Kajiár, through the forest alive with monkeys and resounding with the whistle of the mavis and the call of the cuckoo, and into a steep path lined with jessamine and flowering peach, which brings him to the bank of the river, whence looking up he sees CHAMBA, with its white palace in the centre, and away beyond it a great mountain of snow, at the end of a valley, glowing like gold in the setting sun."

Is it Fairyland? Something at least very like it. Here since 1871 Dr Hutchison has been missionary-in-chief, Mr Carter for many years has shared his medical journeys and his toils, and since 1895 he has had for women comrades the ladies of the Women's Mission. At present these are Miss Kidley and Miss Stanfield. The beautiful church, built and presented in 1901 by the late Rajah for the use of his Christian subjects, schools for boys with 160 pupils and for girls with 98, and two excellent Mission Houses, are our Mission's chief equipment to-day. Year after year Dr Hutchison crosses the snowy passes, and is welcomed as a great 'healer' in the many valleys that lie beyond. Christian influence is well maintained; but unfortunately it has not been possible for many years to post an ordained missionary to Chamba, and in consequence the *Church*, the centre of Christian life, seems to be waiting for that personal push which will come when to the staff of devoted doctor and lay missionary and two ladies working in the Hospital Zenana and the school, there is added a consecrated Christian minister. May it be soon!

A 'Dream Mission' it must remain to us, but happily the leading figures in Chamba are no dreams. It happened that later, when we were in Lahore, the Rajah and the Ranee of Chamba, attended by their trusted friend and physician, Dr Hutchison, were then residing in their Lahore home. By the good offices of the doctor an interview was granted, and my wife had the honour of a long talk with the graceful and courteous Ranee, while I had the same with the young Rajah. Both were thanked in the name of the Church for their kindness to our Mission and our missionaries, and after pleasant intercourse we left. So after all, if the Mission remain a dream, the 'First Family' in Chamba are pleasant realities.

CHAPTER IX.

YOUNGSONABAD—WHERE CHUHRAS RISE AND WALK.

BUT who are the *Chuhras?* They are the hands and the feet of the Panjab, the serfs of the soil, the untouchables of the Indian social system, the humble labourers who are found on the fringe of every village, toiling for the Hindu or Mohammedan dwellers, but themselves profiting not by all their toil. They are the aborigines of the Panjab, descendants of those who occupied these wide plains when first the Aryan invaders came swooping down on India, and defeated and enslaved the people they dispossessed. Through the long centuries that have passed, they have been a people destitute, despised, held down to the very dust, until the possibility of better things ever coming to *them* had ceased to enter into their wildest dreams. They were down, and down they would remain. Yet now to these children of a captivity as bad as that of Israel in Egypt has come a wonderful deliverance. Christian missionaries have said to them, "In the name of the Lord Jesus Christ, arise and walk!"—and Youngsonabad is one of many places where this miracle is seen accomplished.

In our Scottish Mission Dr John Youngson was the pioneer apostle to these children of adversity. Earlier missionaries had concentrated on Hindu and Mohammedan, either overlooking the despised outcastes of the villages, or hesitating to embark on a work that might prejudice their more important enterprises. That now is all a thing of the past; and in the early 'eighties of last century, just forty years ago, it was John Youngson who in the Panjab first had the wider vision. Here and there Chuhras who happened to hear the 'Good News' showed eager interest, pressed into the Kingdom, and would not be denied. These came and brought their brothers also. "This is the Lord's doing, and marvellous in our eyes," said our great "Bishop of the Chuhras," and to its furtherance gave his consecrated strength. The 'School of the Prophets' established at Daska gave him his preachers, and soon in scores of villages Chuhra congregations arose. Tens became hundreds, hundreds grew to thousands, and to-day of the 15,000 Christians in our Panjab Mission, the great majority are from this once despised but now increasingly respected section of the people of the Panjab.

That varied motives were at work in this notable mass movement is undoubted. In Christianity the people long depressed saw a power to uplift them, socially and intellectually, as well as spiritually. A desire to rise and a desire to learn, as well as a thirst for righteousness, have been at work. And who will blame them? Are not all three most honourable aspirations? But that the message of the Gospel finds a congenial home in the hearts of the Chuhra folk beyond anything that Hinduism can show is also sure. For their own ancestral religion is singularly pure, and free from the idolatrous taints of Hinduism. Witness this translation by Dr Youngson of part of one of their favourite religious recitations :—

"Sing praise to God, the great Original
Who sat on waters dark contemplative.
He first, of yielding clay with wondrous art—
As Sculptor wise—began to trace the face
And features, mould the forms and limbs of man.
There Adam lay all lifeless still, without
Or sense or motion, when to the entrance door
Of this new mansion God led up the soul.
The voice of God said 'Enter.' 'Nay!' the soul
Cried fearfully, 'I will not enter there!

In house so dark I could not live!' 'Fear not!'
God said. 'A day will come when I will set
Thee free, and take thee to Myself again.
My word is sure.' Thus urged, the soul in fear
Obedient entered: Adam sneezed and woke,
Pervading soul now quickened every part;
And Adam stood the father designate
Of all the race."

A little Miltonic perhaps in the roll of the verse to be exactly 'Chuhra,' but the content is strikingly pure. And how the richness of the evangel tells, when a *Christian* Chuhra poet strikes the lyre, is seen from the following, often sung at the close of a baptismal service:—

"Bring my Jesus to me, O my God!
To Thy door have I come, O my Creator!
The winner of my heart, Christ the Beloved!
My Creator, my beloved Lord!
Let me never forget Thee, my Lord, O Christ!
'Twas for me He came into the world:
My Beloved lost His life for my soul,
And saved my soul from sin.
I wandered about astray and lost,
But I heard His voice calling me;
Having pity on me, a sinner,
He bore the burden of my sorrows;
He injured none,
Yet the cruel ones crucified Him.
O cruel ones! Why did you commit this dreadful deed?
Did not the fear of God restrain you?
We are all beggars at Thy door,
Thou hast fed us all.
In Thy hand is all my life,
The shadow of Thy mercy is over me.
O Beloved, show kindness to me,
Who am oppressed by many sorrows."

Truly a people whose soul is here laid bare are well worth lifting up, and giving a fair chance to walk erect and honoured through life.

Yet let there be no mistake. Material worth lifting is there in abundance; but the task is not an easy one, and calls for an expenditure of men and money by the Missions concerned that few are fully able to meet. Despite the hopeful spiritual soil, the mental and moral degradation which centuries of servitude have wrought is such that the shepherding of sheep, so long-left friendless, is a mighty enterprise alike of faith and works. To hold them for Christ after the first impulse has brought them to Him, to train them in the knowledge of the Christian faith, to educate them in the most primary of schools, to make them 'literate' to the extent of being able to read the Scriptures in their own tongue, and to fit them to fill well their humble rôle in life, while at the same time giving to their boys and girls of 'pregnant pairts' a chance of rising higher—these are practical problems of the highest moment that face all the Missions that are confronted with the mass movements in their areas of work.

Where the solution is easiest is where the community to be served is gathered at a centre, and not scattered over a hundred villages in groups of ten or twenty. The latter is the usual case in the Panjab, but at YOUNGSONABAD there is a happy concentration, for this is a Christian settlement with a population of 1800 people, all Christians!

It had its origin some twenty years ago. The splendid engineering enterprise of the Government in canal irrigation in the Panjab had brought within possibility of cultivation thousands of acres along the numerous canals that branch from the Chenab river. Applications for allotments were legion, for in India there is no thirst that can compare with the thirst for land. Dr Youngson had a most happy inspiration. Why not apply for a grant of land, and plant upon it a colony of these Christian Chuhras now so eager to make good? All precedent was against land being given to any save the zemindar class, but Sir Mackworth Young, then Governor of the Panjab, saw fit to break with tradition, and land was granted—not to the Scottish Mission only, but also to the neighbouring Missions of the American Presbyterians and the Church Mission Society of the Church of England. Our special settlement was named most fittingly YOUNGSONABAD. Forty-four acres was the whole extent, and this, divided and subdivided, was portioned out to carefully selected settlers, drawn from every part of our Mission Field. That was twenty years ago, and now we were to see to what the experiment in Christian colonisation had grown.

It was from Lahore that we made the journey, but over the experiences of the road it is well not to delay. Journeying mercies were few that day. Along with Mr Scott we started at 7 A.M. in a motor on what was said to be a fifty-miles' run over quite good road. It proved to be sixty-five miles, over a road parts of which could not be excelled for badness, and towards the end the motor got increasingly 'camsteary.' However, finally we reached our destination at 1.30 P.M.—two hours and a half late. At 3.30 we had to leave on the return journey. On the way back the petrol failed, darkness overtook us, and we sat disconsolate, but at last were rescued from a cold night in the open wilderness by the arrival of a swift motor laden with rugs and refreshment, sent out by the kind thought of Sir Edward and Lady Maclagan, whose guests we then were, to scour the country and bring in the missing pilgrims. So all ended well. By 10.30 P.M. we were rejoicing in front of a fire in our room at Government House, exceeding glad that despite everything, we had seen Youngsonabad—one of the finest sights we beheld in India!

Where the side road to the settlement leaves the main road, a great company of the settlers met us, headed by Padre Mark. Truly tumultuous was the joyous welcome we received, indicative of the glad hearts of the Christian folk at this visit from the Mother Church in Scotland. Accompanied by a throng of enthusiastic men and women, boys and girls, which grew in volume as we went on, we moved up the path to Youngsonabad, and with banners waving, fireworks cracking, and dust enveloping us in mighty clouds, we reached the goal. Verily it is a great achievement—a Christian colony now 1800 strong, dwelling in a well-planned village, with fertile fields around, all rich with promise of coming harvest. In the village itself stands a most worthy church, a house for the pastor, and a school for the children, who were circling around in an ecstasy of delight. The seniors of the settlement conducted us to the open space under the shadow of the church, where a great gathering was held. Then came addresses and replies in full abundance. Signs of healthy progress and of promise were nowhere far to seek. The goodly church was built by the settlers themselves; the pastor is supported by their own contributions; self-supporting, too, is the school. But most gratifying of all was the sight of the Christian folk who form the settlement—sturdy self-respecting men and women, who have had a chance of proving their quality and have taken it. The condition of the land is itself an evidence of the settlers' industry and skill; and very pleasing proof of the growth of the spirit of manhood and of manliness was that which was given when the Great War sent its appeal for men through India. Two hundred stalwart men went from Youngsonabad to work in hospitals in Mesopotamia, Palestine, and France; while hundreds more of their brothers from other parts of the Mission Field flocked to fill the ranks of the Christian regiment. Nor are they slow to proclaim the greatness of their debt to the Mission. In Youngsonabad that day the leading note in all the addresses was gratitude for all that the missionaries had done.

Of course there were requests as well for further aid, but not of a monetary kind. Two desires were uppermost, and with both there will be much sympathy. One was for land—more land! The colony is growing rapidly in numbers, and by constant division and subdivision the original portion for each settler is now sadly diminished. In a document presented to me 200 of these sons of toil affixed their names and thumbmarks to an earnest appeal for additional land, sufficient for the growing needs. But, alas! the power to give lies not with the Church, and a Government, sympathetic but impartial, has to deal with many cries of a like kind before responding to any one.

More in the power of the Church is the response to the second cry. It was an appeal for a missionary to be planted in their midst, and if two could come so much the better. For these settlers are ambitious for their children, as any Scottish father and mother would be. So they want a missionary to come and live in Youngsonabad. One they already had for a season, Miss M'Queen, who for five months occupied a mud hut there last cold season, and radiated light and hope and knowledge. "We want her, or another like her, to be ever with us," was the strongly urged request; "and we want Mr Scott or a man like him to live amongst us too." Which is to say, they want the living, helping touch and pervasive influence of two of 'God's own missionaries.' They know that then will come better schooling and other things. No word here of having had enough of European missionaries! They know better, and long for more. It seems to me the very place where, in the absence of an ordained missionary, a good layman and a like-minded wife could do endless service. But that, of course, means a house and other things, and all means money! What money can do is shown by the neighbouring Christian colony of Martinpur, the settlement of the American United Presbyterian Mission. This fine Mission concentrates on two fields —Egypt and the Panjab—and pours out the consecrated dollar and the consecrated worker on both most bountifully. So Martinpur rejoices in a Middle School, worked with efficiency by the Mission, and has a regular system of scholarships by which deserving pupils are transferred to schools where they receive industrial training or higher education, and so are fitted for greater things. Youngsonabad looks on and wishes like things for itself, but first and chiefly a missionary residing in its midst.

Had Dr Youngson lived a few more years the colony that is his best memorial would have got a fresh impulse forward in several ways, for his mind was busily at work regarding these children of his heart at the very hour that God's call came. But his spirit and his love live on in those who follow him, and Youngsonabad will never be left without the tender fostering of the Scottish Mission so long as fostering is needed; and that will not be for very long. Whatever help can be given will be right well bestowed, for the place and people are worthy of it. Never shall we forget the enthusiastic friendship we there encountered, and the gladness experienced on seeing the glowing reality of the uplift that comes to a lowly people when they clasp the outstretched hand of Christ. And this is the written message they sent to the Church across the seas that had been Christ's agent in their redeeming. "Convey our thanks," said Mr Thakur Dass, the leading layman, "to all our benefactors in Scotland. Tell them we are not an ungrateful people. Christ has made us good citizens, loyal subjects of our Christian Emperor, and loving children of God, our Father in heaven. This, sir, is the fruit of your Church's labours in India. For a little longer India needs your assistance and your prayers. A National Church is soon to arise. Sectarianism will vanish, Christ will be glorified, and you will have your reward—a bright jewel in your crown, brighter than the Koh-i-Nur of India."

CHAPTER X.

G.H.Q. IN THE MISSION FIELD.

BEFORE we say good-bye to the Panjab Mission, it is good to spend a few hours at G.H.Q. There we come into touch with the Authority that guides the whole campaign, and in so doing learn something of the difficult problems that are up for solution to-day. At the Mission G.H.Q. there is no Commander-in-Chief; but there is a *Mission Council*, composed of the missionaries, women as well as men. G.H.Q. is wherever the Council meets, and as a rule Sialkot is the chosen centre. Here it was that on 15th November, in the Ladies' Mission House, there assembled one of the most representative Councils ever held by our Panjab Mission. Including the two visitors from home, who represented the two Mission Committees of the Home Church, there were in all 23 members present, every missionary then on the Field being there. Mr M'Cheyne Paterson, with his pacific benevolence which never fails, made an ideal chairman, and in Mr Dalgetty the Council had a wholly admirable secretary. We sat from 10 to 2, from 2.45 to 4, and from 4.30 to 7 P.M. It was a steady day's work, and the work was well and fully done. In all there were seventeen items on the agenda, none unimportant, and several of great importance. Five of these may be indicated, as of more than merely local or passing interest.

1. *The Educational Policy of the Mission* was the first subject for discussion, but the title is a little misleading. Given adequate working strength, no criticism was suggested of the present policy of maintaining a good school at each big centre and a college crowning all at Sialkot. But things had been happening at home and in the Field that made a discussion of the wider question desirable. In Scotland there is shortage of money and shortage of offers of service from suitable men. In the Field there is a rapid extension of the Christian Church throughout the districts, and growing opportunities of a further gathering-in of the outcast. At present every one of our ordained missionaries has a divided activity, part of his strength being given to education, part to the evangelistic work in the surrounding district. In these circumstances would a redistribution of the available strength not be desirable, even though it might mean a lowering of the efficiency of the educational work? Without a dissentient voice the Council declined to approve of any suggestion of this kind. Not at this hour in India's development can Christian education be allowed to suffer. Not less energy in men and money for education, but more energy in both for the evangelising of the districts, and the strengthening of the Indian Church. "We want," said the Council, "*additional* missionaries, who shall be set apart exclusively for the development of the districts, and not tied to any centre with the care of a great school. Should the often-threatened *Conscience Clause* be imposed, and attendance at religious instruction be made optional in every school that draws a grant-in-aid from Government, then the whole question of the continuance of the Mission

schools will have to be reconsidered. But while things continue as they are—and the outlook is less threatening than it was—let us carry on."

2. *A Christian University for the Panjab* was the next big topic for discussion, and truly it is very big. The proposal originates with the people who first dream big things and then do them—the Americans, whose Missions in the Panjab are of great extent and power. As yet it is only a proposal that is being ventilated, but should Indian education become increasingly de-Christianised, a 'Christian University' may speedily materialise. Planted at some suitable centre in the north-west, away from any large city, this University may one day be the copestone of a great independent system of education, worked from foundation to summit by the Christian Missions, without Government aid, and having a charter of its own, even as has already been granted to the Mohammedan University at Aligarh, and the Hindu University at Benares. Not willingly will any Christian Mission see its students segregated from their Hindu and Mohammedan fellow-Indians, but things may happen to render such a course advisable. At present 'opinions' only were being asked for. So the matter came before the Council, and a wise Committee of three was appointed to confer with the other Missions interested.

3. The difficult question of the relations of *Church and Mission* next came up for consideration, and a *modus vivendi* between Indian Presbytery and Mission Council was proposed. But prudently, discussion and decision were left over until a Joint Committee of four Indian members of Presbytery and four Scottish members of Council had considered the whole matter. No other Mission question in India is so keenly discussed in these days as this. In every Field we found it a living

issue, though nowhere quite so 'lively' as in the Panjab.

4. To pass from these high themes to the concrete proposal of a local *Memorial to Dr Youngson* was a welcome relief. The form of the memorial had been decided at a previous meeting. A Youngson Memorial Fund of Rs. 6000 (£400) is being raised by the Indian Christians, with the purpose of endowing a 'Youngson Catechist' for work in the Nankana district. Nothing could be more fitting, and for raising the money the method of 'allocation' had been approved. To each local church had been stated the amount of its suitable contribution, and the money was coming in, only rather more slowly than is desirable. Times are hard, and money is scarce in the Church of the Panjab, as in Churches nearer home. But Dr Youngson belonged to India and to Scotland as well as to the Panjab; and it was resolved to make the modest proposal more widely known that friends outwith the Panjab might take part. He that hath ears to hear, let him hear.

5. No matter discussed was more difficult to settle than that which figured in the agenda as *Location of Ladies*. Several missionaries had returned from furlough, two new missionaries had come, and it was for the Council to decide on the best distribution throughout the Field of the whole staff now available. One has only to imagine the harmony that would prevail at a Presbytery meeting in Scotland should a scheme of periodical redistribution of ministers be adopted, to recognise the ticklish and delicate business that now faced the Council. But it was carried through successfully, and with wonderfully little breeze. "I am ready to go wherever the Council thinks best," was the prevailing attitude. But even so the task was not easy, for qualifi-

cations differ, as also do the needs of places. One conclusion forced home was that in these days, when education is a vital part of the women's work in the Mission Field, the distribution of workers would be made vastly easier if every worker sent out to the Field had some training in educational methods prior to her coming. And another conclusion was as to the need of paying due regard to temperament, when posting two ladies to a station where their fellowship is bound to be almost as intimate as that of husband and wife—and that without their having had the privilege of choice!

Verily an important meeting this at G.H.Q. in which questions of a bigness had to be faced such as in a score of years never once trouble a Home Presbytery. Is it any wonder that the constant pleading from the Field is to send out the very best men and women that the Church possesses?

With the meeting of the Council our visit to the Panjab Field culminated, and the super-culmination came on the evening of the day when, at Miss Plumb's most hospitable and expansive table the twenty-three councillors sat down, a little wearied perhaps with the long and strenuous sederunt, but neither worn nor sad. In happy talk and pleasant reminiscence, as well as with much physical satisfaction, the evening slipped away, and with 'Auld Lang Syne' we rose from the table. Then through to the Council-chamber once again, to sing God's praise, to thank Him for the rich fellowship we had enjoyed, and to offer our united supplication for friends at home, and for the good estate of the Church of Christ in the Panjab.

CHAPTER XI.

LAHORE, MEERUT, AGRA—WITH THE CHAPLAINS.

ON leaving the Panjab Mission Field, the next to beckon us was the oldest of all our Scottish Fields—Calcutta. The journey across the great northern Indian plain from west to east was, however, spread out over a fortnight, during which we were immersed in the work and interests of *Scottish Chaplains.* One felt that it was wholly good that this should be, if India were to be seen in anything like true perspective. India is 'British India' still; and all moderates whom I met, whether they were Indians or British, recognised that it is for India's good that not for a long time yet should 'British' be deleted from the name. 'What God hath joined together let not man put asunder.' Co-operation between the races is a prime necessity. So it was useful from time to time throughout this tour to change one's environment. Missions gave us the company of Indians, and of men and women of European blood whose main outlook was 'Indian' too. Chaplaincies, on the other hand, brought us into contact with Europeans, whose talk and judgments and outlook were affected by their racial inheritance. Both partners in the firm had something to say concerning the conditions of the firm's continued stability and prosperity. From each one gathered 'atmosphere,' and learned the wisdom of looking at India's many problems from more than one side.

LAHORE was reached on 19th November, and from the very pleasant centre of Government House we absorbed, during the next four days, as much of Lahore as possible. Sir Edward and Lady Maclagan, honoured bearers of a name to which Edinburgh has long done honour, were the essence of kindness, and Mr and Mrs Johnston Wright, the Scots chaplain and his wife, were indefatigable in guiding us to the things we most wished to see, and in bringing us into touch with Lahore Scots. It is a great city, and a beautiful one as well. As the capital of the Panjab it has long had a place in history, and its history is not yet finished. Just at the time of our visit things were a bit 'jumpy.' The Prince of Wales had landed two days before at Bombay, and throughout the Panjab a 'Hartal,' or a cessation from work, as a silent protest had been pretty general. In Lahore itself the municipality had shown no exuberant loyalty; indeed, it had lately evoked an animated correspondence in the press, by passing a resolution to remove forthwith the statue of Lord Lawrence from the prominent site it occupies in the chief thoroughfare of Lahore. Happily a higher authority stayed the unworthy action, but there was danger that some hotheads might try to work some damage; and throughout our stay we had the pain of seeing this statue of the 'Saviour of the Panjab,' one of the greatest sons whom Britain has ever sent to India, and one of India's truest friends, guarded by sepoys with bayonets fixed! It was significant of much.

The Scots chaplaincy here serves at present mainly the appropriate section of the civil population, and has as its centre an attractive and well-furnished church, once the care of the American missionaries, but now the property and care of the Church of Scotland. A large congregation assembled here on the Sunday evening, including the Governor's party. The cosmopolitan nature of the congregation was interesting and gratifying. Scots, of course, in the majority, but English, Irish, American, and Indian were all represented—a truly catholic flock. One met them later in a more intimate way at a garden-party arranged by Mr and Mrs Wright in the beautiful grounds of Government House, most kindly granted by the Governor. Here, too, one met representatives of other branches of the Church, Anglican and non-Anglican, clerical and lay, and joyed in the true friendliness that was everywhere in evidence. A good and useful sphere this for a minister of the Church of Scotland, and it is well filled. Nor was the military side of the chaplaincy entirely wanting. No Scots regiment was there, but on Sunday morning some forty Scots, mostly in the Air Force, paraded for service in the hall of the Y.M.C.A. buildings. Should a Scottish regiment come to Lahore, the Garrison Church will have to be obtained for parade service, as 'St Andrew's' is too small and too remote. But some day a Scots kirk suitable for both purposes, and conveniently situated, should arise in Lahore.

Lahore has many sights worth seeing and writing about, but this is not a general guide-book. Three of the notable things we saw must, however, be mentioned —the Aitchison College, the Forman Christian College, and the Kinnaird College for Women. The *Aitchison College* is a magnificent institution, a palatial building in extensive grounds, where the sons of the chiefs of the Panjab receive an education and a training that cannot fail to be of great service in fitting them for the high positions they will one day occupy. Here Mr Kelly is the capable principal, the son of a former minister of our Church; the *Forman Christian College* is the famous college of the American Presbyterian Mission, named after its truly great founder, and carrying on to-day the largest educational work done by any Mission in North-Western India; and the *Kinnaird College* for women, not large as yet, but aiming at a large work, when by the co-operation of all the Missions in the North-West—our own included—it will be the honoured goal of the best pupils from the many schools and high schools where Christian girls are to-day being educated.

MEERUT is a night's journey from Lahore, and when we reached the station on a cold morning at 6.30, we were warmed by the greeting of Mr Jamieson, the Scots chaplain, and further gladdened by the hospitality that waited us at the house of the Judge, Mr Neave. Mrs Hay Neave is a keen friend of the Church in Abernethy and elsewhere. We had only a day here, and I used it by paying a call at the mess of the *Seaforth Highlanders*, visiting some of the congregation, and seeing the church. A new Scots Church is sanctioned, "as soon as funds are available." But meantime in this old building which has its history, the Scottish services are conducted. In Mutiny days this was the theatre. Hard by is the old Garrison Church, where, one Sunday in May 1857, the English regiment was at service, *without their rifles*, when hell broke loose at Meerut and its fires spread all over India. To-day Meerut shows no trace of these old days of tragedy, and as a place to live in is appreciated by soldier and civilian alike.

Next morning, Friday, 25th November, saw us up at 4 A.M., and stealing away as noiselessly as possible from the bungalow of our kind host and hostess, to catch a train for AGRA. Mr Jamieson saw us off, and six hours later we were met at Agra station by Mr Mackenzie, chaplain to the King's Own Scottish Borderers. A gallant regiment is the K.O.S.B., and more than happy the relations of the regiment and its chaplain. Three months later the regiment was to move to Egypt, and regrets at losing its chaplain were already freely spoken. The parade service held on the Sunday forenoon in the large Garrison Church was one of the finest in all our Indian tour. Far off one heard the pipes coming ever

The Taj Mahal, Agra.

nearer, then the great body of braw young men filed into church. The band of the regiment led the praise. Perfect reverence and sustained attention all through the service, and nowhere was it more tense than when words of loving remembrance from the Kirk at home were spoken. Then 'the collection,' taken up by two sergeants, the Benediction, and the National Anthem at the close. Once more the skirl of the pipes, and to the call of a stirring Highland air the brave lads marched away. But not quite all. There was Communion that day, and over thirty remained behind to break bread and have fellowship with Him whose love and power overleap the widest seas, and whose hand was laid in blessing at once on us who bowed the head in India and on our loved ones far away. An officer, two sergeants, and a private distributed the elements, the officer being Major Youngson, son of a well-known Aberdeen elder of the days of my own youth. Alas! since that day of high and holy things at Agra this good soldier of Christ and of his King has died, called home on landing in Egypt with his beloved regiment.

One cannot leave Agra without seeing the TAJ! At least he would be a strange mortal who did so. Throughout this Pilgrimage we had to rule out from our programme the great majority of the 'sights' of the places visited, saying sternly 'One thing I do.' Missions and chaplaincies needed all our time, and they got it, save so much as was required for sleep—tired nature's sweet restorer. But at Agra we made one exception. We gave a day to the Taj, and our consciences never once pricked us for so doing.

Of the Taj what shall I say? Nothing, because nothing I could write would be in the least adequate. In my note-book I find a few ecstatic words—a Dream! an Inspiration! a Poem! and at that I'll leave it. In mass and in detail it is alike incomparable—so far as my experience goes. Description and appreciation are best left to the picture and the poem, and a sample of each is given here. But one does not require to be a poet in order to appreciate the depth of that royal love of long ago, that here has found so rare a setting for all time. It was in 1612 that Shah Jehan of the Moghul line of kings married the lady who is known to history as *Mumtaz Mahal*, "Exalted of the Palace," and for seventeen years the love that bound the two in one was strong and tender and true. Then the breach came. The lady died, but the love endured, stronger if possible than ever, and in her honour the matchless tomb was raised—the Taj Mahal. Seventeen years it took to build, 20,000 workmen were employed in its construction, and the cost of its erection is stated at three crores of rupees, or two million pounds. Evil days came on the bereft husband, for, as the custom too often was in those old times, his son Aurangzeb, getting impatient for the throne, deposed and imprisoned his father in the great Fort of Agra, which had been built by Akbar the Mighty. There, after seven years' confinement, Shah Jehan died. That wondrous fort contains many palaces within its walls, but one of the choicest spots of all is the *Jasmine Tower*, built by Jehangir, Akbar's son, for the occupancy of his famous empress, Nur Jehan. Here later Mumtaz Mahal had spent many of her happiest hours. And hither old Shah Jehan, when he felt that life's closing hour had come, at his own request was carried. The view from the balcony is superb, and has for its central object the great white marble dome of the Taj Mahal. Here, with his eye fixed on the glory-tomb of his beloved queen, and with his soul going out to her with love unchanged, the royal lover breathed his last.

There were great men in that wonderful line of Moghul rulers—great in war, great in love, and often great in statesmanship. Ruthless, too, some of them were in their fanatical hatred of idolatry, and their cruel abuse of their Hindu subjects. But big men for all that, whose mark on India abides to this day, and who have left behind them traditions of Empire that are still a power in India with men of their own faith. Monuments of their greatness are many, but none of all can equal in beauty the Taj Mahal, where Queen Mumtaz and Shah Jehan now lie side by side.

"· · · · · that strange shape of grace
Instinct with loveliness—not masonry!
Not architecture! as all others are,
But the proud passion of an Emperor's love
Wrought into living stone, which gleams and soars
With body of beauty shrining soul and thought,
Insomuch that it haps as when some face
Divinely fair unveils before our eyes—
Some woman, beautiful unspeakably,—
And the blood quickens, and the spirit leaps,
And will to worship bends the half-yielded knees,
While breath forgets to breathe; so is the Taj:
You see it with the heart before the eyes
Have scope to gaze. All white! snow-white! cloud-white!

· · · · · · · · · · ·

Hushed, you advance—your gaze still fixed! heart, soul
Full of the wonder; drinking in its spell
Of purity and mystery, its poise
Magical, weird, aërial; the ghost
Of Thought draped white—as if that Sultan's sigh
Had lived in issuing from his love and grief
Immense, and taken huge embodiment
Which one rash word might change from Tomb to Cloud.

· · · · · · · · · · ·

You enter, reverent—for a Queen is here,
And the dead King who loved her; and Death's self
Who ends all—and begins all: and Love's might
Which greater is than Death, and heeds him not.
White! white! tenderly softly white! . . ."

SIR EDWIN ARNOLD.

CHAPTER XII.

CALCUTTA—WITH THE SCOTS.

FROM Agra to Calcutta took two nights and a day in the train, and it was with becoming respect that we approached the great city which still remains the capital of India. In the official records *Delhi* is now the capital, for is it not for six months of the year the seat of Government, and do not the Honourable Senators who sit in the new Legislative Assembly, devising measures wise or unwise for all India, sit there too? All true, and yet Calcutta remains the premier city, the city which counts most for the prosperity of India. Whether it be in politics or commerce, social development or education, Calcutta leads India. As to whether it is the 'second city of the Empire' or not, that is a question to be discussed with Bombay and Glasgow. All three make the claim, but it is near enough the truth to class them as 'second equal,' each having a population of about one million. . . . .

Eighteen years had passed since last we visited Calcutta, and the huge developments that have taken place since that day overwhelmed one. The "London of the East," the Duke of Connaught termed it on his recent visit, and the comparison is very apt. There is the same sense of the vastness of the city, the insignificance of one's own individual self, the same ceaseless tread of myriads of human beings, and the same mad rush of thousands of motor-cars and taxi-cabs, driven at a rate calculated to slay a hundred daily. Oh for a lodge in some vast wilderness, was the secret desire of one's soul. That was to come in due time—but first the mighty city.

Street Scene, Lahore.

Church of Scotland Staff, Calcutta.

Back Row—Mr Wright (C.), Mr M'Lean (C.), Miss Clark, Mr Drummond Gordon (C.), Mr Ingram (C.), Miss Gasper, Mr Mill (M.), Mr M'Lellan (M.), Mr Cameron (M.)
Front Row—Mrs Ingram, Mrs Ogilvie, Dr Ogilvie, Miss Longhurst, Miss Watt.
C. = Chaplain. M. = Missionary.

For about a hundred years the Scottish Church has been at work here, seeking to serve two widely contrasted constituencies—the Scots and 'Young Bengal.' To see this double work as it is to-day took two solid weeks, every day being packed full with engagements. The first five days were given to the Chaplaincies, the remaining nine to the Missions. In four hospitable homes we were successively happy guests, first at Government House, where Lord and Lady Ronaldshay were exceeding kind, and thereafter at our Ladies' Mission House at Cossipore, at Principal Watt's house in the Scottish Churches College, and at the house of Professor Mill in the same college. Everywhere was kindness, and though four changes of base in fourteen days had its penalties, yet one found it a decided advantage to see things from more than one "inside of the outside."

Nothing could have been better timed than the first contact with Calcutta 'brither Scots.' We reached the City of Palaces on 29th November, and next day was 'St Andrew's Day'! Now everywhere, save in Scotland, St Andrew's Day is to the Scot the 'day of days,' and in Calcutta it is even more so. No other gathering of Scots on this day of national festival compares with that held in Calcutta. Alike in numbers and in importance it comes first. From far and near through all Bengal the Scotsmen rally; and if a Governor or Viceroy has a great declaration of public interest to make, St Andrew's Dinner supplies the favourite platform. In the past Lord Dufferin and Lord Curzon each spoke words here that have a place in history: this year Lord Ronaldshay was to add another to these speeches that count. And as a place for the ambassador of the Kirk, giving his first salute to the assembled Scots of Calcutta, no spot could compare with this. Four hundred enthusiastic Scots and Scotsmen's guests filled the great hall. Lord Ronaldshay occupied the chair, and saw that all things went as all things should. Pipers from the Scots Fusiliers alternated with the Governor's band in giving music such as makes the Scot more Caledonian than ever. There was a hush of expectancy when the chairman rose to give his speech. It was a masterpiece—quiet, measured, emphatic, strong. The Non-Co-operation movement was then approaching a climax, and the Government had at last decided that toleration could no further go. Yet one more offer to the extremists was made. "To the leaders in India," said the Governor, "I offer once more the hand of friendship and co-operation for India's good. Will they clasp it?" When he ceased a storm of enthusiastic applause broke out. Again and again throughout the evening it was renewed, whenever opportunity offered of expressing the unusual appreciation felt for this most popular of Governors.

Among the guests were four Indians—a new departure for St Andrew's Dinner, and a good departure. They were four Ministers of State in the new Government; and to one of them, the veteran, Sir Surendranath Bannerjee, was given the honour of replying for 'The Guests' of all nationalities. His speech was one of rich eloquence; but it was more. In it he took occasion, on behalf of all Indians of moderate mind, to clasp the hand which the Governor had held out; and by a happy instinct he turned ere he closed to eulogise the priceless services rendered to India by Scottish missionaries from Dr Duff to the men of the present hour, testifying, with a break in his voice, that all that was best in himself was derived from his missionary teachers in his early days. My own opportunity came when asked to reply to the toast, "The Land o' Cakes." As a rule this toast is sacrosanct from any reply; but it was felt that the presence of the Kirk's Commissioner, fresh from home, justified the innovation. It was a joy to give to these enthusiastic Scots a message warm with affection and fond remembrance from the old folks at home. The reception of the message was very gladdening, as also was the kind thought that led the band to play, when I sat down, "Will ye no' come back again?" Love for the Kirk is not dead in the heart of the Calcutta Scots. It may go to sleep 'whiles,' but it is there sure enough.

A happy custom has ordained that on the Sunday following St Andrew's Day the secular joys of a St Andrew's Dinner should be succeeded by the hallowing influences of a national Scottish service in *St Andrew's Church.* For such a service no church in the East has the qualifications possessed by the Calcutta kirk. It is more than a kirk; it is a National Institution, which shrines memories of a century-old fight for Scottish rights, when the Kirk had to take off the gloves if she were to have a place in the sun at all. Dr Bryce, the first chaplain, took them off and smote hard. The Anglican authorities of the day in India challenged the right of a Scottish church to have a spire—badge of national status: result, the spire went a foot higher than that of the cathedral! Then the right of Scottish ministers to marry their own people was denied, and—will it be believed?—the Scottish Church authorities at home, for peace' sake, said, 'Let be, let be!' But Dr Bryce would not 'let be.' He fought the pacifists in the General Assembly and carried the day. So, little by little, was it impressed on the high officials in India that Scotland too has a National Church, and will not be denied her national place in any part of the British Empire. The trouble has been that, with new generations of officials, this elementary instruction has had to be given over and over again.

But on Sunday, 4th December 1921, there was no place for dubiety. Their Excellencies, the Governor and

Lady Ronaldshay, were in the Governor's pew, and the fine old church was filled with a congregation of Scots who knew their country's place and the place of their country's Kirk. It was a memorable service. No fewer than eight ministers of our Church were there, five taking part in the service. The old psalms dear to Scottish hearts were sung, the sermon dwelt on the religious notes that Scotland looks for in her sons, and the climax came with the reading of the Assembly's letter to Scottish congregations in the Far East. Interesting, too, to many was the fact that, for the first time in India, the preacher wore the official dress of a Moderator of the General Assembly of the Church of Scotland; and not uninteresting may be this further fact that, before leaving the vestry for the service that night, he who wore the robes faced up before the portrait of Dr Bryce, and bowed respectfully to the Church's champion of a hundred years ago.

In the morning of the day there had been a service of another kind. At Barrackpore, eight miles north of Calcutta, the Royal Scots Fusiliers were quartered, and with Mr M'Lean, the chaplain, assisting, parade service was held in the Garrison Church. There, as always, it was a delight to speak to the Scottish soldiers, though in this regiment Presbyterians are not in such an overwhelming majority as one expects to find in Scottish regiments, but every draft from home was helping to put things right.

One more service with Calcutta Scots was held on the following Sunday evening, in the United Free Church in Wellesley Square, where one was equally at home. A fine congregation gathered; Mr M'Kinnon, the minister, shared the duties, and I rejoiced in being able to give the greetings of the Scottish Church at home to the other half of the Church in Calcutta. Here, as elsewhere in India, our countrymen, and not less our country-women, are ripe for union, and are impatient over the delays at home. It will be a real gain for the churches in Calcutta when it comes. Both the present churches are situated in the business quarter of the city, remote from the residential area. With union there will still be two congregations, for the Calcutta Scots are sufficiently numerous for that; but while one will remain in the historic city, the other will find a local habitation in the suburban area where Europeans most do congregate.

St Andrew's Day and the Sunday services supplied what may be termed official 'contacts' with the Scots of Calcutta, but in between were many contacts of other kinds—Kirk-session meetings; Committee meetings; daily talks with the two chaplains, Mr Drummond Gordon the Presidency Senior Chaplain, valued organiser, correspondent, and friend through this Indian tour, and Mr Ingram, his brotherly junior colleague; a most hearty 'welcome' congregational 'At Home'; many delightful private gatherings of a social kind; and a great official dinner with seventy guests at Government House. In these crowded days one gathered European 'atmosphere' very rapidly; but most of all did I increasingly realise the greatness of the sphere which Calcutta offers for a devoted Scottish ministry, and the urgent duty which lies on the Churches at home in this matter. There is splendid 'fishing' to be done here, but it requires extra good 'fishers.' How sound the heart of this great community is in regard to higher duties is not best judged by counting heads at an ordinary Church service, nor even by considering the high efficiency of the many Church organisations. Better still is such evidence as this: A little while ago our Ladies' Mission, which has its headquarters at Cossipore, away in the extreme north of Calcutta, found it very difficult to arrange for sending the Indian women teachers to the various day-schools throughout the city. The Kirk-session and other Scots put on their considering cap. And now a motor-omnibus is the property of the Mission, which distributes the teachers every morning, and then gathers them up and takes them safe home every afternoon.

Or better evidence still of the soundness of the Calcutta European heart. That noble enterprise, the Kalimpong Homes, like other philanthropies, has times of strain, sometimes pretty severe strain. What happens? Dr Graham comes down to Calcutta, calls a meeting of the mercantile community, tells his needs—and rupees pour in by the ten thousand! Yes, the heart is sound enough.

CHAPTER XIII.

CALCUTTA—WITH 'YOUNG BENGAL.'

SCOTTISH Missions in Calcutta are emphatically Missions to '*Young* Bengal.' 'Old' Bengal is not altogether forgotten, middle-aged Bengal gets a modicum of attention, but nine-tenths of the missionary energy goes to serve the young men and the young women, the boys and the girls who together constitute 'Young Bengal.' Of the nine days we gave to the Missions in Calcutta, eight were occupied with work for the young, or with Councils concerning it. Geographical considerations, rather than distinctions of sex, decided the order in which the many activities were seen, but here it will help to a clear impression of the varied work if the two

Scottish Churches' College, Calcutta.

great departments, as far as is possible, are presented to the reader separately—first the work for the Young Men and Boys, and second, that for the Young Women and Girls.

I.

In any account of the kind, the Scottish Churches College must come first. Its past history, as well as its present work, gives it a premier place. Like St Andrew's Kirk, only in a far greater degree, the Scottish Churches College is more than its name implies: it is a National Institution. It has a place in the history of Modern India. Should Modern India seek for its birthplace, as many claims for the honour would be put forward as for Homer's natal spot—and with greater justice, for Modern India is a very complex organism. It has in truth had many birthplaces. But beyond question one of the chiefest of them all is the original Scottish school, opened by Dr Duff in 1830, whose lineal descendant is the Scottish Churches College of to-day. Here it was that the great experiment was first made of giving a training in the knowledge and Christian culture of the West to the sons of the East. Once the process had begun, it swept like a great conquering stream over the whole land, for India was eager, perhaps even over-eager, for the new wisdom. It gave her new thoughts, new life, new ideals, new ambitions, and little by little new power. To-day we see to what it has all grown, and while there may be some things that were better unseen, there can be but one opinion as to the immense advance that India has made in her mental and spiritual equipment since Western knowledge and Christian teaching began to be poured out for her acceptance. From Duff's day to the present hour, the Scottish Church has not wavered in its endeavour to win the soul of India for Christ, by giving to her youth an education penetrated throughout with Christian influences. In Calcutta the endeavour has grown from more to more. In 1837 the humble school gave place to the stately 'General Assembly's Institution' in Cornwallis Square. In 1843 came the Disruption, when Dr Duff and his colleagues began work anew in the Duff College, while the Assembly's Institution carried on, after a brief *hiatus*, under Dr Ogilvie. For sixty-five years the divided work continued—two Scottish missionary colleges working in Calcutta, in rigid though increasingly friendly independence,—and then came in 1908 the healing of the breach. Economic considerations gave the spur to Christian unity, and the Mission work of the two Scottish Churches in Calcutta—the women's work excepted—was unified under the name of the *Scottish Churches Mission.* The Duff College was sold; large additions were made to the original institution; and now the noble *Scottish Churches College* stands out as a sign of Scottish unity, and as the crown of Scottish educational missionary effort for India's people.

Come and see the College at work. Along one of the crowded main streets of the city we are whirled by a reckless taxi-driver, every inch of ground being occupied by buildings or vehicles or human beings, and no sign of any academic grove presenting itself. At last a break in the monotony: on one side of the street a well-kept lakelet with ornamental surroundings, and on its farther side a noble stretch of buildings, manifestly an original centre block with later additions, and (as subsequent acquaintance shows) solid extensions to the rear, right away to the parallel street behind. This is the Scottish Churches College. The Rev. Dr Watt, the present principal, who has filled the post well ever since Dr Wann's day, meets us at the entrance, and guides us for a whole forenoon over his impressive kingdom. There are some 900 students at work, and a staff of

40 professors, lecturers, and assistants, 9 being European missionaries. The nine missionaries ought to be twelve, but three of our own Church's posts are at present waiting to be filled.

It is 10 A.M., and for fifteen minutes we have a very pleasant talk with the Indian professors in their common room as they arrive for the day's work, which begins at 10.30. They are a striking body of young savants. The average age is about thirty years or thereby. All are keen men, interested in their work and in life, and, like all men of their class in India to-day, very keen in things political. A not unhealthy nationalism crops out again and again in the talk, but as the time of our visit is rather a 'hot' time politically, a prudent avoidance of the hottest topics marks the conversation. Now, as all through our Calcutta visit, it is a real pleasure to meet these young intellectuals, and, I think, not a one-sided pleasure only.

At 10.15 the bell rings for the opening service of prayer, held in the large hall. Attendance is voluntary, but hundreds of young Indians are present, and with a hymn, Scripture-reading, and prayer by Mr Cameron, the work of the day is launched. Thereafter comes a series of visits to the many spacious class-rooms where the students are at work; and it is good work. Class after class is seen, and kindly words of greeting spoken. Every class without exception is in perfect order, and instruction is being ably given by Indian and European teachers. English, Philosophy, Mathematics, History, Economics, Science, practical and theoretic—every branch is cared for, and as the University examinations show, both the sowing and the harvesting are good.

And what of Religious Instruction? At one o'clock every day the students are gathered into nine large classes, and for half an hour very definite Bible knowledge is imparted. Come to the class taught by Dr

Watt. Some 230 students crowd the benches. The passage dealt with is that which tells of the healing of the palsy. Dr Watt expounds with fulness and frankness. Christ as the healer of the body and the soul of needy man is exalted. The Gospel note rings true and sounds out clear. Verily the missionary aim of the College is not minimised.

But apart from direct instruction in the truths of Christianity, the influence of Christian personality and the power of Christian contact are continually in exercise. Probably this is most of all the case in the five *Hostels*, in each of which fifty to sixty students are housed, and are in daily intimate touch with one or other of the leading Christian members of the College staff. Each Hostel has its own life and interests, and nourishes its own loyalties ; but in all character-building is a primary aim. On the morning of my second Sunday in Calcutta, I was taken to the Tomory Hostel for a short religious service at 8 A.M. All the resident students were Hindus, but there were fifty present, and no more alert congregation have I ever addressed on the Christian rule of life than I did that day. Without doubt, for the higher life of the students, these Hostels, under sympathetic supervision, are of first-class importance.

For long Indian colleges suffered, like our Scottish Universities, from over-absorption of the students in their studies ! In the students' estimate of life nothing else mattered, save to work up and pass the examinations prescribed. Students as a class were 'grinders'; colleges, with rare exceptions, were education-mills. Their specific *missionary* aim helped to rescue Mission colleges in some degree from this hurtful limitation, but not altogether ; and in them, as in other colleges, there has been during the last twenty years a marked advance in the attention paid to the non-instructional side of student life. The Scottish Churches College has been a leader in this healthy development. Sports have now a real place in the thought and life of the College, and an excellent playing-field of six acres extent (where we witnessed the annual sports, and my fellow-pilgrim gave away the prizes), supplies the needed area for the manly contests that do so much to form manly men. For mental gymnastics that help to widen the outlook of Young India, College Societies exist which in number and in variety rival the Universities at home. To serve the whole man—body, mind, and spirit—in the best possible way is the aim of this truly great College.

The main feeder of the College is the *Scottish Churches Collegiate School.* This is under the enthusiastic management of Mr W. Alexander, aided by a staff of over thirty teachers, nearly half of whom are Christians. It, too, is a noble institution. Situated at a little distance off from the College, it has a life and reputation of its own. One thousand boys are in attendance, and the building is worthy of this eager young army. Three-storeys high, each storey has seven thoroughly good class-rooms, while attached is a two-storey annexe for the elementary department. Everywhere is life, energy, and enthusiasm, and a ready willingness on the part of the management to launch out along any line that promises to benefit the boys. One instance of this is the starting of a class in practical telegraphy. Boys are selected for this by examination, receive their training, and are sure of a Government post when their course is completed. Truly a fine school, where building, staff, and pupils are all up-to-date, a worthy memorial of the days when Principal Lamb was at the wheel—and this was the first notable building resulting from the union of the Missions.

The climax of this part of our Calcutta visit came with the celebration of College Day on 9th December, when, in the grounds adjoining the College, there was held the annual distribution of prizes, and the annual delivery of speeches. An unusual element was supplied by the unhappy prevalence of political excitement at the time, and the consequent uncertainty as to how the attendance of the students at the function would be affected. Some of the prominent Congress leaders, heroes in the eyes of Young India, had just been placed under arrest for their open support of Non-Co-operation leading to violence. The Indian press was seeing red, several schools and colleges were deserted by their pupils in token of protest, Calcutta looked as if it might be 'nasty,' and streets quite near the College were being patrolled by British soldiers with machine-guns. Not a very peaceful environment for a College Day Prize Distribution. For a time the students gathered slowly, but outside the gates they were seen in crowds. Why not enter in? Because the police party who were regulating the orderly packing of carriages, &c., were in charge of a European sergeant, and only when the man of offending racial authority disappeared did the Indians freely enter! Such was Calcutta in December 1921. In the end the gathering was large and entirely cordial. Dr Watt read a most gratifying report for the year. My wife distributed the prizes to a great number of smiling recipients, and the function closed with "God save the King." Two speeches were given, one of exceptional interest being by Sir Deva Prasad Sarvadhikary, C.I.E., who had just returned from a visit to all the Universities of Britain, and who now took occasion to extol the hospitality shown by the Scottish Universities to Indian students as compared with that of the Universities of England, and recommended his young hearers to choose Scotland if they should cross the seas for further education. My own words from the chair, spoken in gathering darkness and with multitudinous crows chorussing around, dealt with the past of the College, and with the growing importance of the service which missionary colleges have it in their power to render to the New India of to-day. Truly it is incalculably great. Never have the alumni of these colleges had so much real power in their hand for the shaping of their country as they now possess. Never was it more urgent to shape the 'shapers,' so that they may do their great work well. And, may I add, never has the College been more devotedly served by great-hearted missionaries than to-day, and never did it offer a finer sphere for Christian service than in this hour of India's transformation. Who volunteers?

II.

To see the *Women's Work* of our Mission in Calcutta, within a limited time, you must hire or borrow a motor. Happily the kindness of motor-possessing friends—notably Sir Alexander Murray, the Mission staff of the College who own a motor in common, and St Andrew's Kirk itself—supplied all our needs. But the motor which was a necessity for us is also a necessity for the Mission ladies, if their work is to be done without regrettable overstrain. In the old days it was not so necessary. Until 1911 the base of operations, the Ladies' Mission House, was located in the very heart of the great city, at "125 Bow Bazaar," and work done in the north or in the south extremities was not unreachable. Now the Mission House is situated in Cossipore, at the extreme north end of the eight-miles-long metropolis; and to work the south from the north demands a motor,—at least until, as is contemplated, a second Mission House arises in the South End, and the staff of missionaries divides.

To the ladies we were indebted for a very pleasant social gathering of missionary friends belonging to all the Churches, which served as our introduction to 'Missionary Calcutta.' It was held in the spacious compound of the Mission House on a beautiful afternoon in the beginning of December—when all the afternoons in India are beautiful. English, Scottish, American, and Indian friends were there from many Missions, and then, as so often in India, one realised with gladness the striking unity that marks Christian Missions to-day in India. The Mission House is a commodious building with many rooms, where are housed not only our six missionary ladies, but also a number of the Christian teachers, who are occupied during the day in one or other of the City schools. It is at once a happy home and a strong base of Christian service.

School work is of three varieties, and we saw them all. First, there are schools of the kind adopted from the start by our Mission, and whose importance is still undiminished—viz., *Schools for Hindu Girls*. Of these, there are four in the northern half of the city, hidden away out of sight, and reached only after much twisting and turning along the narrow crowded streets. To these schools in succession we were conducted one day by Miss Longhurst, the experienced and devoted senior missionary. Their regular supervision is in Miss Laha's competent hands. To the little pupils, as to us, the visits were a great event. They were as anxious to exhibit the extent of their knowledge and the variety of their accomplishments in sewing, embroidery, modelling, drill, singing, and Scripture knowledge as we were charmed to see it all. The buildings may in several cases be not up-to-date, for they are mostly rented Hindu houses, which means insufficiency of room and light, and tortuous modes of access; but the instruction is thoroughly good, and it needs little imagination to realise what these few years of bright and happy school experiences mean for the enrichment of the whole life of these little girls, soon to be burdened with women's duties, cares, and sorrows. Specially delightful was it to witness the eagerness with which Bible stories were retold by selected pupils. They were born tellers of tales, and though one was ignorant of the language in which the excited narrators spoke, yet the eager eyes, the self-forgetting gestures, and the eloquent rush of words declared how the story possessed the tellers. So eager did some become that they got mastered by the rush of words, gulped down what threatened to be a choke, and sped on with the tale! Be sure these tales are told and retold in very many homes. And in the long years in front of the eager speakers, the lessons of these stories they know so well will come again and again to cheer and strengthen in the hard places of life. From 100 to 140 girls filled each school—from 500 to 600 of India's maidens daily receiving instruction that makes them useful daughters of their country, and learning such things of the love of God as will bring gladness to their hearts as long as life lasts. Is this not a service right well worth rendering?

Akin to these schools are three schools of a rather less-developed type that we visited another day away at the '*South End*' *of Calcutta*, near the great docks on the Hooghly, where the interests of the sea have brought together a large population—in KIDDERPORE, MATHIABRUZ, and BUDGE-BUDGE. About 100 girls were present in each school; but most interesting of all was Budge-Budge, a rural centre some seventeen miles away from Calcutta. In itself it is an interesting attractive spot, but for us its importance lies in the fact that here will likely be the future base of the Women's Work on the South Side. The whole of this district is marked out as its sphere of 'District Work' by the Scottish Churches Mission, and one visualises in the near future two Mission Houses in this area—one for the 'District' missionary of the Scottish Churches Mission, the other occupied by two ladies of the Women's

Mission—and the allied work radiating out into the country surrounding, to the glory of God and the well-being of the yet unshephered people. Already at Budge-Budge the Mission has a good Boys' School, under a most capable young Christian headmaster, Mr Daniel, and a district church with an Indian minister at Mathiabruz. With adequate supervision it is safe to prophesy no small things for the work at the 'South End.'

Beyond question, however, the fairest flower of the Women's Mission is the *Boarding School for Christian Girls* at Cossipore, where, under the vigorous and capable management of Miss Clark and her colleague Miss Watson, eighty Christian girls are housed and fed and trained in all good things and ways. It was the dream of this fine institution arising that mainly drew the Mission from the centre to the suburbs. Now the dream has been splendidly fulfilled, and it was pure joy to us to witness its fulfilment. A long two-storied range of buildings, fronted by deep verandahs, and looking out on a small field of green grass; an ideal school the lower storey, an ideal dormitory the upper, an ideally secluded playing-ground the green sward in front. And, it may be truly added, an ideal management.

Guided by Miss Clark and Miss Watson, we spent an afternoon in going over the whole school, saw the various classes of bright intelligent girls with a look of happy ease in their own position that betokened good things for their future, and an absence of the over-timid shrinking that one had often noted in non-Christian girls. At the close of the 'inspection' all gathered in the fine large hall, and with songs and action songs, recitations, speeches, and *garlands*, the happy afternoon came to a happy close.

It is one of the best bits of work in the Mission. These girls are to be the wives of Christian men, and in many cases the teachers in Girls' Schools. They are to be 'mothers in Israel,' and in the training they are getting here lies a goodly part of Israel's hope.

Over and above all this school-work there is the teaching, secular and religious, carried on in zenanas by Miss Watt, Miss Gasper, Mrs Bose, and numerous Bible-women. This was a closed region for me, and lack of time made it also a closed region for my wife. But as a following-up of the seed-sowing in the Hindu Girls' Schools it is impossible to speak of it too highly.

III.

In most Mission Fields a fair indication of the past effectiveness of the work of the Mission is given by the condition of the Indian Church within the area. If the Church is found to be rooted and grounded in the heart of the people, an organism alive and extending with visible rapidity, it is a safe conclusion that the work of the Mission has been sound. If the Church be weak and non-progressive, the Mission has surely suffered from some defects. This easy test, however, has its limitations. For general 'District work,' where the upbuilding of an indigenous Church is the 'chief end' of the Mission, the test is not as a rule unfair; but where the 'chief end' of a Mission has been of a different nature, the test is of little use. This is the case with the Scottish Missions in Calcutta. There, rightly or wrongly, 'Church-building' has not been the primary end in view. From Duff's time until to-day 'Nation-building' describes better the central purpose—the students and alumni of the college being equipped with Christian principles and strengthened in capacities that will make them true and good leaders of their people in their day and generation. All the Missions of the Reformed Churches in North India have benefited by the 'output' of this Scottish College, which has served the Churches along this line in a remarkable degree. But so far as the Indian Church in Calcutta is concerned, the Scottish Missions have not a great contribution to show. They have in the city itself only one fully-equipped congregation, and the Christian community connected therewith numbers about 600. But it is a congregation of no mean importance, for the *Duff Church* has probably the most influential Indian congregation in the whole of Calcutta. Until 1920 the two Scottish Missions had each their own Bengali congregation (both under the Presbyterian Church in India), the Church of Scotland having 'St Andrew's Bengali Church' and the United Free Church the 'Duff Bengali Church.' Now they are united, the Duff Church being the House of God for both communities, entirely self-supporting, and controlled by a Kirk-session thoroughly alive to its duties and importance. On the forenoon of Sunday, 11th December, when the service in English was held, I preached to a most striking congregation, entirely Indian, with the exception of the missionaries. In front a great cohort of Christian girls and young women from the United Free Church Boarding School, behind sat the regular Indian congregation, to whom English was a familiar tongue, pew after pew being filled with cultured Indian men and women, and behind them a large body of students. The large church was completely filled, and a service comparable in every respect with that of any of our city churches in Scotland was held. Reverence, decorum, heartiness in the praise, keen attention to the sermon—all were there. From a Scottish point of view this was the service which showed a cultured Christianity most impressively of all I had experience of in India. One felt indeed that it was almost too Scottish, and not sufficiently Indian; but in these days in the great cities of India services have to be adapted to the many stages and varieties of culture which the Christian community shows. Earlier in the day, for those whom Western culture had not touched, a full Bengali service had been held, with Bengali hymns and music; and if another section of the community find they worship God better through more Western media, why not make provision therefor? After all, in India to-day English is the language used and British are the models followed in all assemblages, political or social or religious, where Indians trained in Western culture meet together. So let the Duff Church go on being all things to all men, and make provision for the religious outpouring of the soul of cultured and uncultured alike. In speaking afterwards of the remarkable congregation to a ministerial brother (of the United Free Church), he remarked: "Yes, they are a fine people, and they know it. They are the 'United Free St George's' of Calcutta."

One regret I had that forenoon, and only one. The girls of the Church of Scotland Boarding School should have been there too; but it is impossible. Cossipore is three or four miles away, so the girls get a short service for themselves. But it is not the same. Soon, however, there may be a car extension to Cossipore and beyond, and then, for young as well as for adults, Duff Church will be the church of the whole of the Scottish Churches Mission in Calcutta.

IV.

The last forenoon of our Calcutta stay was marked by a delightful visit to the two chief schools worked by the Women's Mission of the United Free Church—the Christian Girls' Boarding School, and the Duff Higher-Grade School for Hindu Girls. Our welcome from our United Free Church sisters here, as everywhere in India, was as cordial as heart could desire, and the work was right well worth seeing. The *Boarding School* in Duff Street, adjacent to the church, is run on the same lines as our school at Cossipore. A fine three-storey building provides good accommodation for about 100 girls, who are well supervised by Miss Plumb. But the 'sight' of the Mission is undoubtedly the *Duff School for Hindu Girls.* The buildings are the most entirely adequate to the needs of girls' education of any that we saw in India; and for this, thanks are mainly due to the vision and the tireless push of Miss Hogg, who is in charge. Over and over again in India one has felt how much more up-to-date the Hindu *Boys' Schools* of the Missions are than is the case with the schools for the Hindu *Girls.* In the large cities, while the instruction given in the girls' schools is thoroughly good, too often the school buildings leave very much to be desired. Humble places, hired houses up side-streets, Hindu dwelling-houses never meant for schools, too many of them are. True, things are steadily improving; but in this *Duff Girls' School* we have a perfect model of what one would like to see in every city. A few years ago the old inadequacy prevailed, and then Miss Hogg tackled the matter. The site of one school, which had ground adjacent, was selected for a central school; the land adjoining was acquired; money was raised at home and in Calcutta; and now this palatial building, three storeys high, forming three sides of a square, with open ground in front, and an array of spacious class-rooms, is thronged every day by some 400 Hindu girls, who are being educated in surroundings that are equal to those of the best Boys' School that India can show. Two other schools of the older type still continue, but this is *the* school. May it prove the pioneer of many!

Of the happy meetings wellnigh every evening, with

missionary friends and with friends not missionaries that marked our Calcutta stay, nothing can here be said, save that they were very many and very happy, and extremely helpful too in widening one's knowledge of men and women and things. It was one of the busiest fortnights in one's life, and looking back upon it and remembering the multitudes of things seen and learned as the days glided swiftly past, one pronounces it one of the richest fortnights as well.

CHAPTER XIV.

SERAMPORE—A LANDMARK OF A NEW AGE.

MISSIONS in India do more than live: they grow. With growth come developments that create new needs; and to supply these needs new ways have to be devised. While in Calcutta we were brought into contact with one notable example of this,—a landmark that denotes the arrival of a new age, a development that is charged with benediction, not for one Mission only, but for all the Missions—the *Serampore Theological College.* The name may not sound very seductive, yet the thing signified is full of interest. But come and see, and then pronounce judgment.

Where and what is *Serampore?* It is the old Danish settlement, thirteen miles up the Hooghly, where in 1799 William Carey, Britain's pioneer missionary to India, along with Joshua Marshman and William Ward —a magnificent triumvirate,—began their epoch-making work in India. Calcutta would not receive them. The British authorities of that day would have deported them back to Britain as dangerous disturbers of the peace of India. So in Serampore, under the protection of the Danish flag, and with the avowed support of the Danish king, the good work began; and now for all time Serampore is a leading Christian shrine in India—a hallowed spot, where it is good to remember the days that are gone, and to bow the knee in gratitude to God for His faithful servants of long ago. To-day, however, it is more than the great past of Serampore that draws us there: it is also the great present, and, as I believe, the yet greater future. So to Serampore let us go.

But how? By rail would be the quickest way, but there is a far better way than that—*by River*. And for us the better way was made possible. By the kindness of His Excellency the Governor, and through the brotherly offices of Mr W. R. Gourlay, I.C.S., his Private Secretary and devoted Scottish Churchman, the Governor's fine launch was put at our disposal for the day; likewise a most ample supply of good things for the physical comfort of his guests, also skilled retainers to see things done decently and in order. So on the forenoon of a perfect day, accompanied by Mrs Ward, wife of the Hon. Justice Ward, a true daughter of Glasgow, and Mr Drummond Gordon, our Senior Chaplain, we two pilgrims got on board, and sailed away up the noble river, on what we now look back upon as perhaps the excursion of most serene enjoyment in the whole long tour.

A noble river is the Hooghly, albeit only one of the mouths of the Ganges, and to sail smoothly up the broad expanse of water, continually passing native craft of all varieties of build, and rejoicing in the ever-changing beauty of the river banks, was a sheer delight, as well as a most welcome relaxation. The number and the imposing character of the jute-mills that one passed was a revelation of the extent and importance of this great

Scripture Class, Scottish Churches' College, Calcutta.

The Girls' Boarding School, Cossipore, Calcutta.

industry. Here it is that the Rev. Mr Wright's extensive parish, or county, is situated. There are some thirty-five of these mills scattered up and down the river, each with its band of resident Europeans, varying in numbers from ten to a hundred. They cannot come to church, so the church goes to them, Mr Wright and his United Free Church colleague going up and down the river on Sundays, and holding services successively at all the mills. It is good to remember that these 'Mills and Steamer Chaplains' are provided by the Companies that own the mills—a kindly considerateness for their employees that is much appreciated by the men and by the Churches with which they co-operate.

Very noticeable too on the banks are the numerous beautiful villas owned and occupied by Indian gentlemen. Evidently the quiet repose and beauty of the river-side appeals to the East as much as to the West. Hindu temples are frequent, of a more restrained type of architecture than is common, some of them with long rows of cells for the occupancy of devotees of their gods. Farther up we pass on the right the old circular deserted temple in which Henry Martyn, a hundred years ago, made his home, still known as 'Henry Martyn's Pagoda,' and carefully preserved by an appreciative Government. But Serampore is now getting nearer, and after an *al fresco* lunch has been enjoyed, we approach the ghat where is the landing-place, and step ashore—to be met by an old friend of twenty years ago. This is Mr Burns, a descendant of a collateral branch of the family of Robert Burns. Twenty years ago he was a boy in my church at Madras, and now, hearing that his old padre was coming, he brings his motor-car to convey us swiftly to the College. It is a welcome touch with the old days.

Soon we reach the College, to be met and cordially welcomed by the present distinguished principal, Dr

Howell. It is a stately building, or rather range of buildings. The old Grecian-fronted block, with its great flight of steps and its pillared portico, which dates from Carey's days, is as impressive as ever; but vast additions have been made since then, most interesting of all, from my point of view, being a fine quadrangle with ample hostel accommodation all round for the students. First, however, to the Library of the College —Carey's Library! Here we are on holy ground, for we touch the books that Carey touched, open the books that Carey wrote, admire the numerous translations of Holy Writ that issued from the busy Mission press, the Bible in Chinese being added to many issues in the Indian tongues. Here Carey lived and worked, and up yonder in a room not far off he died. Verily it is good to be here: the great past envelops us.

But what of the present greatness? There is an Arts Department in this College with over 300 students, but this is not what we have come to see. What is unique here is the *Theological Department*, where some thirty students are in residence, drawn from every part of India, owning allegiance to more than half a dozen Churches, and all pursuing here a three years' theological course, ending with the winning of the degree of Bachelor of Divinity. India has no other College of which these things can be said, and the story of how they can be said of Serampore is something of a romance.

In 1827 this institution was incorporated by Royal Charter granted by the King of Denmark, and given University powers, under the control of an independent council. In 1845 Serampore was purchased by Britain from the Danes, but the charter was confirmed as a thing inviolable. Long years passed and no exercise of the degree-conferring right was ever made, until in general it was forgotten. Now, however, there comes along this new century of ours, when the Indian Church is producing men who are keenly athirst for higher training, but who for University recognition in theology must go to Britain. Degrees in other faculties can be won at the Indian State Universities, but there is no faculty of Christian Theology in these. Then it was that Serampore, seeing the need, awoke to its own potentialities. "Here," said the Baptist missionaries, "is what India wants for the higher training of her Christian ministers. Let us widen the basis of this old College, let us invite the other Churches to co-operate, let us make a catholic Council representative of all, and let Serampore take its place as the Theological College for all Christian India." Wonderful to tell, it has all been done; and the Indian Church is being steadily enriched by the emergence from this old-young College, so rich in memories and in hopes, of Indian theologians, trained in a manner equal to their brothers of the West, and stamped even as they are with the mystic letters B.D.

Later that day we visited the students, and saw their comfortable study-bedrooms and their spacious common-room. They were delightful young fellows from many parts—North India, South India, Ceylon, Central India, and several from Malabar. Denominationally they were equally diverse—Syrians, Anglicans, Baptists, Presbyterians, Congregationalists, and Lutherans,—all loyal to their own communions, but learning here in the best possible way how real and overmastering is the wider unity of the one Church of the Lord Jesus Christ.

All praise to our Baptist friends for their wide outlook and most catholic action. They are doing a great service here for the Indian Church. But they must not be left to bear the burden alone. Assistance from other Missions they have already in some measure received. Bishops' College of the Church of England has helped in lectures, and so has the Syrian Church; but they desire and deserve more. Help in men or money is asked, especially help in men; and the hope is cherished that some day the 'Scottish Churches College' may spare them one. That day has not yet come, but things are happening in India to-day that may hasten its coming and do even more. The vision of a Christian University at Serampore, cherished by Carey and his colleagues, is not abandoned by their present-day successors—a "University conferring its own degrees, not only in Theology, but in Arts, Science, and Medicine." But they add when they write of such things: "We realise that only princely munificence on the part of one or more men of great wealth could make the fulfilment of such a vision possible." Yet stranger things have happened, and this great dream may one day be realised.

All too soon this memorable visit came to a close. Down the river we sailed, enjoying once again the rich placid beauty of it all, and rejoicing greatly over all that we had seen. At 5 P.M. we reached Calcutta, and so ended an Elysian day.

CHAPTER XV.

THE TEA-GARDENS OF THE DUARS.

A FORTNIGHT had been spent in Calcutta, and the call from the Eastern Himalayas had become imperative. "On your way here, however," wrote Dr Graham, "*you must visit the Duars.*" It was difficult to get it squeezed into an already full programme, but when you are approaching his kingdom, J. A. G. must be obeyed, and a visit of thirty-six hours among the tea-gardens was arranged.

It took some travelling. On the afternoon of Tuesday 13th December, we took train at Sealdah Station in Calcutta, and left with a hearty handshake from our latest hosts, Mr and Mrs Mill and Dr and Mrs Watt. The train was a beauty, quite the best we sampled in our many Indian journeys—sleeping compartments, dining-car, and a smoking-lounge for those of both sexes who desired the weed,—being ahead of the arrangements in most of our home railways. The Eastern Bengal Railway does things well. Unfortunately we had to leave this travelling palace all too soon. On the journey we dealt with several junctions bearing weird names—Santahar, Lalmonirhat, and Mal—before reaching CHALSA, our goal, which we did at 1.30 P.M. next day. At Mal a very kind friend, Mr Haig, cousin of the Field-Marshal and an equally good Scot, jalousing that we would need refreshment, had made abundant provision, which, as our only repast that day had been a cup of tea and no bread at 6 A.M., was gratefully welcomed. But a station before Mal had given us grand refreshment of another kind. Into our carriage stepped Dr Graham of Kalimpong, my lifelong friend, and his charming daughter Miss Betty! They had come down into the Duars by a back-door from Kalimpong, and were here to meet us. It was a joyous meeting. A little whiter on the top than when I had last seen him, eight years before, but to that one gets reconciled. Much work, many anxieties, and deep deep sorrow had been his portion of these years, but also much sympathy and abounding help; and here he was—the same hearty, kind, boyish, big-souled human as ever. The Duars work is one of his many pet enterprises, and he rejoiced to show its points. From the station a motor took us rapidly through splendid tea country, all trim and beautifully bounteous with innumerable tea-shrubs, to the *Matelli* estate, where in the bungalow of Mr and

Mrs Carmichael we got a welcome that kings might covet.

Here must be inserted two notes—one geographical, the other historical. The DUARS is a richly fertile district, which extends for about a hundred miles along the base of the foot-hills of the Eastern Himalayas. On the northern side of these hills lies Kalimpong. The average width of the district is twenty miles, and the greater part of this, which thirty years ago was a favourite haunt of elephants, tigers, and other big game, is now covered with Tea-gardens. The population has three elements: the planting community of two to three hundred Europeans, predominantly Scottish; thousands of Indian coolies, who come from various parts of India to work the gardens; and yet more thousands of the aboriginal inhabitants, known as the Mechis. So much for geography.

As to history: the district lies within the sphere of the Eastern Himalayan Mission of the Church of Scotland, and its 'Church history' really began when, some thirty years ago, Dr Graham commenced to pay occasional visits to the district, and got into touch with both European planters and Indian labourers. That there was a great sphere here for a Scots minister who would be both a missionary and a chaplain was convincingly clear; and twenty-three years ago (1899) the Duars Missionary Chaplaincy came into existence, thanks mainly to the energetic push of Dr Graham, the fine co-operation of a number of the planters, and the willing help of the Scottish Companies who own many of the estates. All these years the planting community have never failed to raise some £300 annually towards the necessary salary, and the Church of Scotland has supplied a fine succession of ministers, among them being Duncan Macmichael; well-beloved T. E. Taylor, who gave his brave young life in this service; and Peter

Milne, who, after a ministry of sixteen years, highly acceptable to the planting community, and grandly blessed in the ingathering of the Mechis, has lately returned to Scotland. And the result? This at least: a community of Scottish men and women who have the kindliest feelings towards the Kirk, who welcome the minister with both hands whenever he comes round, who in many cases support a missionary evangelist teacher on their own estates for their coolies, who in several instances have built humble churches for the Christians, and who in wellnigh every case second any endeavours the Mission may make for the benefit of the indigenous Mechis or the Indians from afar. And for those same Mechis, timid, kindly, intelligent children of the forest, what is the result? A mass movement towards Christianity, which is seen in a Christian community of 3700 souls; and perhaps best result of all—the fostering of a sense of kinship in the religious life between the Indian employed and the European employers. Prior to the date of our visit there had been a *hiatus* in the ministry—always an unfortunate occurrence. Now, however, a fresh start was being made, and Mr and Mrs Giles, the new minister and his wife, had just arrived. To help to start them well was an unlooked-for pleasure.

Our first contact was with the European 'parishioners,' the planters and their wives, and it could not have been more happily timed. It was 'Tennis afternoon' at Matelli when we arrived. Over forty guests were there from all the neighbouring estates within a radius of at least ten miles. I never wish to see a happier throng of Scots and English residents in India or anywhere else. At once, strangers though we were, we felt at home, and fell in love with the community. Manly men and womanly women of the best type were they all. One almost envied the new minister and his wife their sphere of work. But the climate! Yes. Time was when the Duars had a bad name for climate and sickness—and not without cause. But that time is past, and in all India you will not find a company of Europeans in better health than those we met that day. Clearing the jungle, swallowing a daily pellet of quinine at breakfast-time, and particularly making the houses mosquito-proof by filling doors and windows with fine wire-netting, have worked miracles. Said a Darjeeling planter to me somewhat humorously: "Yes, the Duars are healthy enough now, but I don't fancy spending my days in a meat-safe!" Witty, but not very wise. The said 'meat-safe' is very comfortable, and if health be preserved, and the daily work is duly done, what more do you want?

Our second contact was with the *Indian* parishioners, or rather with their pastors and teachers. Twenty-five of these from the different centres gathered on the following morning at their new 'chief's' manse, and along with Dr Graham we met them there. It was my first meeting with the workers of this north-eastern corner of India, and I was greatly struck with their appearance, square stolid faces, but with intelligence, independence, and character writ large upon them. I gave them a message of regard and encouragement from the Home Church, Dr Graham interpreting; and at once their faces lit up, and they interjected exclamations of warm thanks and appreciation. There was no doubt as to how much they valued this personal touch from Scotland. With true Eastern courtesy they would not let their visitors go with empty hands, and insisted on presenting to my wife a large roll of silk woven in the district. Their gratification at the lady's reply quite eclipsed anything that I had evoked.

Later in the day came another gathering of especial

interest. Back to Mal we went by train, and there halted. A little way from the station was the local club, where a planters' meeting had been convened to give me an opportunity of meeting and addressing them; and by an adroit arrangement a parade of the local squadron of the Northern Bengal Mounted Rifles had been ordered at the same place and hour. This is the volunteer force, all Europeans, on whose promptitude and courage much may depend in these troublous times. So we had a first-class gathering. Mr Giles was introduced and got a good welcome; and for me to follow on with words of warm remembrance from the old land, true appreciation of the sustained help they had given to the best of causes, and an assurance of the confidence felt at home in their doing as Britons should if ever trouble arose, was exceeding pleasant. Nor was the last remark out of place, for their brothers in Assam had just had, and were to have again, their quality in danger tested and proved. The planters' reply was as cordial as had been my own greeting, and it was with an exceeding warm feeling of brotherliness towards the men and women of the Duars that we said good-bye, and made for the station. Will it be believed? The train had been detained for an hour and a half that this meeting might be held! Most hospitable and considerate Duars!

Still another experience worth recording. The rail brought us to Barnes Ghat, which lies on the left bank of the Teesta river. On the right bank of the river is Jalpaiguri, where by another line we were to travel to Siliguri, the station at the base of the Darjeeling Hill Railway. But the distance across is one and a half miles, and the river is broken up into four streams, with three sandy islands between the streams. So to cross it means seven small journeys—boat and trolly, boat and trolly, boat and trolly, and at last a bridge! Tedious but interesting; and at the end of it all came a characteristically kind Scottish welcome from our host for the night, Mr Lees, the Commissioner of the Jalpaiguri District, a relative of the late Dr Cameron Lees of St Giles'. By him next morning we were sped at an early hour upon our way to Siliguri—the base for the journey to the everlasting hills.

CHAPTER XVI.

SCALING THE HIMALAYAS—BY TRAIN!

THE journey we were now to take is one of the most beautiful in the whole world. From Siliguri, our starting-point, to Darjeeling is some fifty miles; to Kurseong, our immediate goal, it is thirty miles. But while Siliguri is on the plains, Kurseong is 5000 feet in height, and Darjeeling is over 7000 feet, so the climb is serious. But done as we did it, it is a luxury. To travel by the ordinary train of the Darjeeling Himalayan Railway gives a rare feast of spectacular delight, but we two pilgrims fared yet better. The 'Rail-Motor,' in which the great ones of the Company make the journey, was put at our disposal by the kindness of the Manager, Mr Addis; and along with our good friend Mr Duncan, who had come down from Darjeeling to meet us, we started on this glorious excursion. Great windows filled the four sides of the motor. Everything that was to be seen lay open before us. And how much there was to see! Continually as we ascended the vegetation changed its character, as also did the temperature.

First, thick impenetrable jungle on either side, the pathless abode of tiger, bear, deer, and wild hog. Then slowly the trees of the forest appear—oak, acacia, fig, with clumps of gigantic bamboo continually recurring. Still higher ascends the line of rail, twisting, turning, reversing, and each angle turned reveals new beauties. Peach, almond, and chestnut show up at 4000 feet; and from 5000 upwards the magnificent tree-ferns of the Himalayas. All the time that this botanical paradise is displaying its beauties, the glories of the mighty mountains are being increasingly unveiled. Spur after spur of the lower ranges, and ere long such panoramas of the giant heights above and beyond as awe one into silence. Our sensations are similar to those experienced on visiting the Taj, that masterpiece of man's creating—only infinitely deeper and greater now, for we are looking on masterpieces from God's own hand. First, ejaculations; then—silence. So much is there to see and to admire that it is almost a relief when, after three hours of exhausting delight, Kurseong is reached.

Now all this glorious country lies in the district of the Darjeeling Mission; hence it was that Mr Duncan so kindly met us at the frontier station of his vast diocese. I have spoken of the glories of Nature so lavishly spread out before us as we mounted ever higher; now let me tell of the victories of Grace that gladdened us all the way. They began at Siliguri itself, where on the station platform we found gathered to meet us some fifty school children of the Mission, with their parents and friends and their Indian padre. A truly delightful company they were, with their chubby faces, impassive at first, but lighting up in a broad smile which remained to the end—as soon as they realised that the visitors from afar were quite human too. It was our first introduction to the new races we were to meet—Nepalis and Lepchas,—and the contrast with the Indian peoples of the plains struck us much, and struck us more and more as the next two weeks went on. Kindly words all round, genial and competitive hand-shaking, and with a parting cheer we were off to scale the mountains. All along the line of rail little communities of Christians are now established, with their little church and their school, their teacher and their evangelist—the 'parishes' of this wonderful district. And on the way up wherever we halted there were waiting at the stations to receive us enthusiastic groups to bid us welcome. At TINDHARIA was the largest group, for this has a larger population, the chief workshops on the line being here. One hundred bairns were assembled, each waving his or her little paper flag. Behind them crowded the older folk, buxom women and stocky men, all, young and old alike, with 'welcome' written on broad smiling faces, and pressed home by a grip of the hand as eloquent as any parish in Scotland could give. Hearty words of goodwill were spoken from the folk in Scotland, the bairns' hearts made glad by little presents for 'sweeties,' that are appreciated there as here; and then, with three ringing cheers, we were sped along our journey.

KURSEONG is an important place, both from a railway point of view and from that of the Mission. It is the headquarters of the railway, and in itself that draws a considerable population, both Indian and European. It is also the gathering centre for the planting community whose estates are on the middle and lower southern slopes of the mountains. In our Mission organisation it is an outpost of Darjeeling, but now has grown so important as to have a Mission establishment of its own—an ordained missionary when things are normal, and one or two lady missionaries; and in each case a staff of Indian assistants, preachers, teachers, and Bible-women. We had a day to see its many interests, and from the railway station, where Miss Henderson and Miss Crompton met us, we were hurried at once to the *Girls' School*, which was closing that day for the holidays. There the whole school was assembled in the open play-yard for a prize distribution and an exhibition of their accomplishments: about 100 pupils, mostly girls, but with a minority of boys, whose parents clamour to get them in for the excellence of the teaching. Regular country lads and lasses they were. Give them a slightly, but only slightly, fairer skin, and you would be excused if you said they were from Perth or Aberdeen! Something, too, of this impression is no doubt due to their good thick clothing, which deprives them of the elegance of their flimsier-clad brothers and sisters on the plains, and makes them more akin to the country youth of old Caledonia. The teachers and the children had been allowed to plan the proceedings of the hour themselves, and truly they did it well. Two well-known tales were 'acted' with great vigour and enjoyment—'The Three Bears' and 'The Prodigal Son'! The part of the Prodigal was in capable hands, and none of the crowd of onlookers is likely to forget that Parable or its teaching. Another new thing here, which impressed us during our whole stay on the heights, was the superior voices of the children when they sang. The shrill tones familiar on the plains gave way to softer, more melodious notes far up here on the heights. The singing of 'I to the hills' to a chant that sounded old Gregorian was a perfect treat.

From the school to the Ladies' Mission House for lunch, and then came two interesting functions with the two sections of the community, Indian and European.

First, the Indian. On the other side of the main road from the Mission House is the church, a chaste edifice, one of the many legacies that Dr Kilgour left behind him in the Darjeeling Field. Here in the fine open space in front the congregation had gathered, and we had a first-class picnic—tea and buns and talk and laughter. And it was real laughter: no make-believe. These Himalayan folk are a fine people, with whom you can talk and jest and laugh just as happily as at home. They enjoy it as much as you. Thereafter we moved into the church, where there was prayer, speeches of welcome, and exchange of affectionate greetings, the Indian pastor being eloquent and cordial to a degree.

After the Indian 'social' came the European 'at home' at the club, where over a score of the residents, planters, railway officials, and civilians came to bid us welcome at the invitation of two ardent Scots Kirk ladies and great friends of the Mission, Mrs O'Brien and Mrs Lennox. It was all a very pleasant evidence of what has been an outstanding feature in our Himalayan Mission from the beginning, the warm cordiality between the Mission and the European residents. Darjeeling was to show it on a larger scale, but here at Kurseong it was delightfully in evidence. And it grew increasingly evident as the evening wore on, and we mounted by rickshaw and 'dandy' to the beautiful home of Mr Addis, the manager of the railway, and invaluable friend to the lady missionaries and their work. Plans for a new school that he had himself prepared were here examined, and things missionary formed the staple talk of the evening. Happy the Mission Field where such friends abound! Kurseong is the centre of a wide district, with a Christian community of over 500—and many more to follow, and with such good friends that we were loath to leave it.

But our motto was 'Excelsior,' so the morning saw us in the train for Darjeeling. Again the wondrous, ever-changing panorama of loveliness, growing in grandeur the higher that we rose. Again at the halting stations the delightful bands of children, waving flags, their faces radiant with smiles, and giving endless salutes and cheers of friendship. So it was that, with nature's glories encircling us, and amid a human atmosphere of friendship and gladness that moved one's heart, we came to DARJEELING—the loveliest and the grandest of all the Mission Fields of our Church.

CHAPTER XVII.

DARJEELING—GIRT ABOUT WITH MAJESTY !

YES, girt with majesty, and with surpassing beauty too. I do not believe this world holds a fairer spot than Darjeeling. The great mountain panorama is unsurpassable in variety and grandeur, while every little spot in the near vicinity, where nature has had her will, is adorned with a prodigality of leaf and flower and grassy slope that baffles adequate description. Look to the south: down on the lower hills rich with the gleaming green of the tea-gardens. The landscape is broken up in striking picturesqueness by recurring mountain spurs, on which are dotted the planters' pleasant bungalows. Your heart leaps with delight at the feast of beauty that lies before you. Look to the north: far up, shooting high into the sky, you see the grandeur and the glory of Kinchinjunga. It is forty-five miles distant, but in this clear atmosphere it looks but ten. Forty miles in length is that mighty battlement, forty miles of spotless snow and ice and glacier-field, sun-bathed in the glorious sunlight—forty miles of fairyland. Little wonder that from the hot parched plains thousands of Europeans, and Indians too, flock here to be invigorated. With a temperature never over 80° nor under 30°, and with a scenic beauty that is itself a continual restorative, it is the most frequented hill station in all India. Here the Government of Bengal come for the hottest months, here schools for European children abound, here every tourist to India finds his way for a brief glimpse of glory—and here for fifty years, and a little more, the Church of Scotland Mission has been established. Thrice blessed are those who find their life-work here.

Now it is about time for a little prose—only it would be unpardonable to write about Darjeeling without first doing obeisance. Who are the people who dwell in this fairyland whom the Mission seeks to serve? Frankly, they don't look at all like fairies, but they are fine folk for all that — the happiest, cheeriest, most brotherly souls we touched in all India. They haven't the beauty of face and figure that is frequent in the dwellers on the plains, particularly in those of high caste, but they have a comeliness that doesn't rub off. They are not a deeply philosophic people, turning out a large body of intellectuals; but they are 'all there,' and they are producing, in these days of greater opportunity, sons and daughters who are proving that their capacity is as high as that of any in India. They are not, as a rule, troubled much with politics, but they know when they are well off, and live in peace with all men. Yet when they are roused, most men fear their wrath—for this is the land from which *Gurkhas* come.

Three races occupy the district, and to all three the Mission operations extend. The *Lepchas* are the original people of Darjeeling, not overfond of work, lovers of the country rather than of the city, shy and retiring in their habits, but a pleasant amiable people to get on with. The *Nepalis*, on the other hand (to whom belong

A Congregation of Women at Kurseong.

Eastern Himalayan Mission Council.

Back Row—Dr Graham, Miss Hebbington, Miss Crompton, Miss M'Intosh, Miss Henderson, Mr Lakshman Singh, Miss Clark, Mr Giles, Dr Cousins, Mr Ferrie, Mr Ogg.
Front Row—Miss Gauld, Mrs Ogilvie, Dr Ogilvie, Hon. Mary Scott, Mr Duncan, Miss Berry.

the Gurkhas), are a manly vigorous race, good agriculturists, a prolific people, who now constitute the chief element in the population of Darjeeling. Like the Lepchas, they are short thick-set folk, but with a stronger character and a keener desire to get on. The *Bhutias* hail from Tibet or Bhutan, and both men and women are well-set-up, of a good stature, and a more than good breadth; capable, independent, kindly folk they are—one of the best of the Himalayan races, who, whether as traders or crofters, hold their own with anybody. The Lepchas' religion may be described as Demonolatry; that of the Nepalis as Hinduism, touched with Demonolatry; that of the Bhutias as a degraded Buddhism. A fine constituency for a Christian Mission to serve; and in addition to it there is also the constituency formed by the large European settlement, which our Mission has gladly served from the beginning of things.

The centre of the Mission's operations is the spacious 'compound' or grounds, where the various Mission buildings are congregated. Happily the site is beautifully central, and possesses one of the very best bits of level ground in all Darjeeling. The town clings to the mountain-side, and steep are the paths that link the various houses and localities together. Specially valued, therefore, is a stretch of level soil. On the little plateau are the Mission Houses for men and for women, the Offices, and the Girls' School; likewise trim garden plots, with roses and many varieties of flower, and the girls' playing-ground. Below is the beautiful church, St Columba's, and the Turnbull Memorial School for boys; while a little farther up is the 'Union' Church, also at the present time in the Mission's charge. Two ordained missionaries, Mr Duncan and Mr Reid, and two lady missionaries, Miss Berry and Miss Henderson, form the present European staff, assisted by a numerous band of Indians.

On arrival at the railway station at noon on Saturday, 17th December, we had a glad welcome from Miss Berry and all the local Mission workers, but were swiftly carried off by Mr Duncan to the Mission House, where for four delightful days we were his guests. The time was short, but its occupations had been skilfully planned.

That afternoon there was an 'At Home' for the Europeans, and for two hours a succession of charming friends came and talked, and tea'd and went. Not Scots only nor Scots Kirk only, but Anglicans, Methodists, Norwegians, and Americans—one large happy family. They were of the permanent residents of Darjeeling, for it was the coldest season, and visitors from the plains were few. Winter clothing was a necessity, and fires were indispensable, but the warmth of the welcome left nothing to be desired.

The Sunday experiences showed us the various elements in the Indian Christian community. First came a great gathering of 230 Sunday School pupils in the hall of the Turnbull School, for prizes, certificates, and addresses. Here one met that grand old man of the Mission, the Rev. Ganga Prasad Pradhan, the ordained Nepali minister—baptised in 1874, later the honoured assistant and colleague of Mr Turnbull and Dr Kilgour in translating the Bible into Nepali, and still the active minister of the Nepali congregation. His years are over the threescore and ten, but he is hale and active still. Future generations will honour his name as that of the first Nepali who gave to his countrymen God's Word in their own tongue. The youngsters who were there that day would have done credit to an Edinburgh Board School. Their singing was vociferous, and in coming up to receive the prizes they had won (among these being several Bibles from the Scottish National Bible Society), there was the same eagerness on the part of the young boys and girls and the same awkward shyness in the bigger ones as is familiar at home; likewise the same sturdy capable look on the faces of all. They have with much truth been repeatedly described as the 'Scots of the Himalayas.'

In the forenoon the church was filled with a Nepali congregation, very impressive in their numbers and their reverence. Communion followed, celebrated in a manner worthy of Home, and at the organ sat Alice Pradhan, the sweet Bible-woman, and daughter of the Nepali Bede.

Service over, we had a walk with Mr Duncan through the Bazaar, for Sunday is the great market-day of the week, and truly it was a polyglot babel of sounds that accompanied us all the way. Evening brought another fine congregation, the Europeans, and it was a treat to preach to them without an interpreter. Altogether a rich Sunday, giving telling testimony to the Mission's good work for young and old, for Indian and European alike.

The general operations of the Mission follow the usual well-proved lines: a Boys' Middle-English School, with 140 pupils, in the Turnbull Memorial Building; in the town and throughout the district, 34 Primary Day Schools and 30 Night Schools, with a total roll of over 1300 pupils; medical dispensary work at two leading centres; fine Sunday School work; and regular services for Europeans, as well as services for the Scottish soldiers, who throughout the summer are to be found in large numbers at the military sanatorium in the neighbourhood. And in addition the literary work, in which Mr Duncan is ever doing something—a big something just now, for a revised Nepali Dictionary is just ready for the Press.

The work of the *Women's Mission* is equally varied—a good Boarding School, with some 40 Christian girls;

attached to it a spacious hall, and some not too spacious rooms, where another 100 girls from the outside come also for their education; 6 out-schools in the town and district: altogether over 500 girls receiving a Christian education. Our visit coincided with the grand exhibition at the end of the year's work, and it was a great occasion.

The town-hall had been lent for the demonstration; for the municipal authorities are vastly appreciative of the value of the Mission. Indeed an interesting partnership in education between the civic authorities and the Women's Mission is just about to be launched. A fine new school for girls is being built by the town, to be managed by the missionaries; and all that the numerous Indian friends saw at the exhibition that day must have convinced them that the town was doing a wise thing. Over 200 girls were present, all pupils from the Boarding School or the Mission out-schools in the town; and the spacious floor of the great hall proved a splendid place for the proceedings. Miss Berry was in her element, supervising this annual climax of her beloved work. First came a Christmas hymn, a short prayer joined in by all, and then four young girls stepped forward and repeated with perfect accuracy the whole of St Luke's narrative of the birth of our Lord. Charming 'gospellers' they were, and many a time will that Gospel be retold. Then games, marching, hopping, graceful gliding; thereafter prizes and short speeches, everybody being pleased, the young pupils most visibly so. They have a winsome naturalness about them, these daughters of the mountains, that draws one's heart to them at once. There is a marked contrast to the non-committal attitude so often met with elsewhere in India; and as for anything like racial antagonism here, there is no sign of anything of the kind. Peace and concord are everywhere. O happy Darjeeling! One more

Darjeeling and Kinchinjunga.

evidence of this. Before the bairns left that day, from a gigantic Christmas-tree in a corner of the hall every little one received a present, the gift of a planter's good lady, Mrs Clothier, the Mission's 'Children's Friend.'

On Tuesday, 20th December, we were up before six o'clock, getting ready for the journey to Kalimpong, twenty-seven miles off. The journey now can be done in one day by the aid of a motor—still a novelty here, where most of the roads are not suited for this mode of progression. But for the first thirteen miles it is now quite feasible. Thereafter it was by rickshaw to Pashok—most hospitable of bungalows, where Mr and Mrs Lister and their clever little daughter Topsy entertained us royally. Miss Topsy, aged five, showed me the marvels of her doll's house, and discoursed gravely on the qualities of the many inhabitants, gollywogs included. I listened entranced, and was rewarded on saying 'good-bye' by being told, "I wish you would come back again!" From Pashok the rickshaws took us down a steep road to the Teesta river, and from there, crossing the beautiful bridge, seven miles in 'dandies' saw us to our journey's end. The whole journey from Darjeeling is one of unexcelled beauty, and the dominating feature of all is the magnificent view of Kinchinjunga! Everest may be the King of the Himalayas, but surely Kinchinjunga is the Queen. Nor is her stature much less than that of her royal partner. If Everest reaches 29,000 feet, Kinchinjunga rises to 28,000; and for impressiveness Everest is not in it. It rises from the centre of the plateau, its base already high and lifted up. Kinchinjunga is seen rising from the Teesta valley, an elevation of only 1000 feet. Looking northward from that road to Kalimpong, one's eye follows the mighty mass up and up, range beyond range, a steady ascent of vision, until the towering summit in its snow-white glory at last is reached. Has the world got another unbroken view of such an elevation?

Slowly moving up the zigzagging road on the other side of the Teesta we had got near to a great jutting corner, when a loud 'Cooee' made us look up. On the crest of the spur was a well-known figure, whose hand was vigorously waving a welcome. It was Dr Graham, the prophet, priest, and king of Kalimpong, making us 'free' of all his grand territory, and in another half-hour we were comfortably settled in the comfortable Mission House of KALIMPONG.

CHAPTER XVIII.

KALIMPONG—'POWER STATION' OF THE EASTERN HIMALAYAS.

KALIMPONG has probably a wider fame throughout Scotland than any other of our Indian Mission stations, and there is good reason for this. It is more than a Mission: it is a whole group of Missions. Other stations have got behind them the warm interest and the proportionate support of the Home Church, and so has Kalimpong. But it has in addition the enthusiastic backing of no less than three special sections of the Church's membership—the Young Men's Guild, the Woman's Guild, and the Universities' Missionary Association. It rejoices therefore in many lovers; and the outpouring of love's offering, in men and women and money, has made Kalimpong a centre of successful extensive and intensive missionary work, which it was a joy to behold, and is now an added joy to record.

In 1903 my wife and I had previously visited the Mission, and even then it was marked out for greatness; now greatness is visible on every side, and Kalimpong, in sober truth, has become the 'Power Station' of the Eastern Himalayan Mission.

The choice of site made by William Macfarlane, the devoted pioneer of the Himalayan Mission in 1873, has been amply justified. Spreading itself out on one of the lower spurs of the Himalayas, Kalimpong, at a height of 4000 feet, has an ideal climate—never too hot and never too cold—and an ideal environment. Billowy hills and sharp-crested mountains abound, but the ground is more of a plateau than either Darjeeling or Kurseong. There is ample room to expand—for agriculture, for building, for fresh outposts,—such as these other stations, clinging to the steep mountain-side, sigh for in vain.

At the heart of Kalimpong lies the wide-stretching Mission demesne, and to those who in early days secured such ample space for expansion the Mission owes a lasting debt. Buildings abound—the commodious Mission House, the beautiful Macfarlane Memorial Church (since 1921 more beautiful than ever by the addition of the fine chancel), the Charteris Hospital, the Girls' School, the Ladies' Mission House, the Girls' Hostel, Robertson Hostel for Boys, the Training Institution, the Allan Manse, and several others, with all of which we shall presently make acquaintance. The impression given is that of an unusually splendid Mission settlement, and the impression is correct. Nothing seen at any of our other stations in India compares with this in the wide range of its operations, and the rich provision made for carrying them on. We had one week to take it all in; we could with profit have given it thrice as long. But the packed programme arranged for every day secured that we saw something of everything. To tell it here in unbroken sequence, following the ceaseless daily march, would be bewildering. It is necessary for clearness to present the great work in sections.

I. THE CARE OF THE SCOTTISH GUILDS.

The District is extensive and very varied in its character. Away to the south, at the foot of the mountains, we had already seen part of it—the *Duars*, where at sixteen centres Indian teachers or catechists are shepherding 3700 Christians and gathering more. From there the main field runs right away north and ever up. On the west the Teesta river marks the boundary between the Kalimpong and the Darjeeling Districts. On the east lies Bhutan, to the north Sikkim, and north of that Tibet. In this district there are 2600 Christians living in 16 'parishes,' organised on the Scottish model, each with its humble school and little church. Indian pastors, catechists, and teachers have all this in their hands, 'superintended' by Dr Graham. Time forbade our going into the District, but, as we shall see, the 'District' came to us—at least the District workers did. Of first importance is the teaching and preaching that is done in these villages. And, let me add, the heroic work of district visitation that is carried on, year in year out, by the Hon. Mary H. Scott, D.C.S. No one comes closer to the life of the villagers than she. The women and the girls of the hills rejoice to see her coming. She is their proved and trusted friend.

Medical Work centres in the *Charteris Hospital*, and radiates out therefrom through the whole district in times of need. But in January, when we were there, the health of the countryside was good, so the staff were at the centre. Dr Ethel Cousins was in charge, her new colleague, Dr M'Donald Smith, not having then arrived. Sister Clark and Sister Gauld headed the nursing department; and of Indian members of the staff there were an assistant surgeon, two nurses, several nurses in training, and a number of 'dressers' and compounders. Quite a large establishment, and it needs to be, for in the 'sick' season the wards are thronged, an average of 900 in-patients being treated every year. Dr Cousins' high reputation for skill, and the nurses' for kind carefulness, will always keep this average on the rise. For long the accommodation has been too limited, but now it is to be improved. At present the two wings of the hospital are occupied by male and female patients respectively, while upstairs are the nurses' quarters. Already, however, the walls of a new hospital building are rising, to which the women's wards will likely be moved, and nigh to it a good Nurses' Home is soon to be built. One afternoon it fell to me to lay the foundation-stone, and it was with peculiar pleasure that I learned that the new building is to bear the name, "The Ogilvie Nurses' Home." One could not wish for a better perpetuation of one's name than this. In acknowledging and accepting the honour, I told the large company that gathered of a visit I paid to the Deaconess Hospital in Edinburgh when I was Moderator, and of a fine tribute rendered to the nurses by a humble Scottish patient. "I used to think," said he, "that it was only in heaven the angels lived, but I was wrong. We have them here beside us every day!" So do the humble hill-folk think of the white-robed ministrants who tend them in the Charteris Hospital, and I should not be surprised if the Nurses' Home gets the fairer appellation of the "Home of the Angels."

The *Education of the Girls*, and the excellent provision which is made for it, gave us great delight. In scope it ranges from elementary instruction of the little tots to the turning out at the other end of excellently trained teachers, fit and keen to carry the light that has enriched their own lives into the surrounding districts. The school 'plant' consists of two long parallel lines of excellent buildings, with a grassy slope between. The upper is the older building, now devoted to the infants and the juniors; the lower is new, and holds the fine class-rooms for the senior pupils, and also for the teachers in training. Miss Smith, whose special charge this is, was on furlough, but her place was admirably filled by Miss M'Intosh and her junior colleague, Miss Hebbington. The whole arrangements are a joy to see. These chubby-faced, purpose-like, happy smiling maids of the mountains, eager to show you how well they can 'say their lessons,' make you feel young again yourself, and the quiet reliable look of the many teachers (themselves trained here) is itself a testimony to the solid work that goes on. The high level of attainment reached by the young teachers in training is a revelation of how things have grown in India. The work of one of these, who had just gone off to Tibet to teach, was shown us, and it was simply splendid. Here were her books of drawings from nature, her notes on her various studies, her notes of method, all in perfect order, and written with a fulness and a neatness that would give her a place among the foremost at a Home Training College. What it must mean to have such trained teachers going out into the schools of the country-side, imbued with a love for their work and a love for their Lord, needs no telling. With rare exceptions all these teachers are Christians. Nowhere in India, not even in the great cities, have we seen a finer bit of Christian educational training of women and for women than this in Kalimpong.

But school alone does not make girls thoroughly fit to be the women their future homes will need. Even in

Scotland this is now being recognised, and although a degree for Housewifery has not yet been established, training in that most necessary faculty is getting increasing consideration. Yet I doubt if Scotland can show anything so practical in this direction as is seen in Kalimpong. Of these girls whom we have just seen at school, sixty-five are boarders in the Mission Hostels. Come and see how things are done in the Hostel, where most of the older girls are housed, adjoining 'Lal Kothi,' the Ladies' Mission House. Round a small square enclosure are the rooms. Each room has five occupants, and these five form a family. Each family is responsible for its own housekeeping. One rupee per member is the allowance per week. Every Saturday the marketing is done, and provisions for the week laid in. Accounts are carefully kept. All the cooking, washing, cleaning, &c., are done by the girls. Going round the rooms we did not find one that was not spotlessly clean and tidy. Surely an admirable training for life this! Yes; and here is another preparation. Every day, before the school-work begins, the girls have an hour and more in the industrial department (of which more anon), where some little skill in a helpful industry is obtained. Culture of mind and soul, perfecting of hand and heart, practical judgment in the economy of a home—all these ingredients are mixed in the rich cup of training that is supplied by the Mission to the happy maids of Kalimpong.

II. THE CARE OF THE SCOTTISH UNIVERSITIES.

"You are invited to breakfast to-morrow at 8 o'clock with Mr Ogg and his boys!" This was our last injunction on retiring for the night of 20th December—the day we arrived at Kalimpong. Accordingly, next morning by 7.30 we were making our way to the higher levels of this extensive settlement, where the Scottish

Universities' Mission challenges the admiring gaze of those who dwell below. Here at the entrance of the Training Institution—a long two-storey building with three projecting blocks—we were met by Mr Ogg, the new principal, who has taken the place so long and worthily held by Dr Sutherland. Like his predecessor, Mr Ogg is an Aberdonian, and like him, too, will 'make good.' Our introduction to the life of the place was refreshingly original. Some fifty sturdy youths were gathered round the breakfast-tables, and at the head of the large room was the principal's table, where we sat. Grace said, the meal began. Great porringers of rice and dhal were in front of the boys, and soon disappeared. We, too, shared this favourite dish in moderation, and something added thereto. A word of greeting to the boys followed the meal. We had broken bread together, and now were friends.

At 9 A.M. the whole school assembled in the 'Constance Taylor Memorial Hall'—a beautiful memorial to a beautiful soul, daughter of Dr Cameron Lees, young wife of Edward Taylor. Two of the best and fairest whom the Church has ever sent to Kalimpong, and both called Home to God in the flower of their youth. Their bodies rest side by side in the little graveyard, but their work goes steadily on. In this hall, which commemorates their name, we met the boys. Over 200 were there, a very striking company—about 150 Nepalis and Lepchas, 50 boys from Bhutan, a few from Tibet, and one or two Chinese. Praise and prayer opened the day, Mr Ferrie, the capable head-master of the school, conducting the service. To his kind help I was then indebted for an interpretation of a brief address, in which I urged the boys to prize and profit by their school-days, and through all their days keep God before them. Then the round of the classes, where boys and teachers were busy and happy. The juniors meet in the lower hall of the

St Columba's Church, Darjeeling.

Darjeeling Bazaar.

adjoining Robertson Hostel, the senior boys and the students in the room on the lower floor of the Institute. In both buildings the upper storeys are devoted to hostel accommodation, where cubicles for the young men and small rooms for the younger lads are all well arranged. Specially interesting were the fifty Bhutia boys—big, strong, athletic fellows, who are to be men who count in Bhutan a few years hence. Not so long ago Bhutan was one of the three 'closed' lands. Now these fifty lads attend school in Bhutan for six months in the summer-time, taught by a teacher from the Mission; and in the cold months they migrate here with their teacher, to be for six months boarders in a Christian hostel. They are not Christians, but how much it means for them and for the future of Christianity in Bhutan, that here and now they are being penetrated by Christian ideas, and shaped by the loving hands of Christian missionaries!

Nor is it teachers only who are here being trained, but theologians too, for Mr Ogg has several budding preachers in his hands, to whom he is imparting sound theology. And for forty years and more this work has been going on, only now it is on a larger scale than ever. It is from Kalimpong that all the schools in the great field are staffed with men and women teachers; from here that all the catechists and pastors issue forth; from here that the large proportion of the boys who are to make their way in Government service, in trading, or in farming, step out into the world. Verily this *is* the 'Power Station' of the Eastern Himalayas, and those who are creating, evoking, and directing the power have one of the finest callings open to man or woman.

Away to the north the Universities' Mission works its own wide district of Sikkim, where there are 350 Christians. Here Mr M'Kean has toiled for long, and opened the way for others to follow. No time had we for a journey north, but one had a very real gratification in having talks with Lakshman Singh, the worthy pastor who is at present in charge. The missionaries want an ordained medical missionary for this field, and with Lakshman Singh as colleague, and the faithful staff of teachers now in the field as supporters, things should go. Again, who offers ?

III. THE KALIMPONG INDUSTRIES.

Behold a tiny seed become a great tree, whose branches shelter a whole people ! The seed was a happy inspiration that came to Mrs Graham away back in the 'nineties, when she bethought herself what she could do to start cottage industries among the crofters of the district, and began to teach a few of the women how to knit and crochet, and by industry add something both to their happiness and their income. The great tree is represented by the multifold Industrial Establishments which have come into being since then, and are now one of the leading features of the Mission. But they are Mrs Graham's work : the Church at home has as yet done little more than smile most benevolently on a great enterprise that has needed no help from Scotland. And it will remain Mrs Graham's best memorial. Come with us as we make the tour of the chief establishments, housed now in imposing buildings, some the gift of a generous Indian friend, others a memorial of the foundress of it all.

Here is the *Lace School*, or rather Lace Factory, for this is serious industry on a financial basis. Years ago there was secured a skilled lady from England to give the skilled training, and now girls and women come freely to the school for instruction. Soon their work pays for their board. A little later they go back to their homes, and the lace pillows, on which most beautiful lace is made, are to be seen in scores and scores of homes. But here at Kalimpong is the centre where the training is given, the material is distributed, and the high quality of patterns is maintained. Now follow the lead of Miss Graham and her colleagues, Miss Korb, Miss Borritt, and Miss Pryce, and pass on into the *Embroidery Department*. Women and girls are hard at work, profiting by an industry first introduced with the help of Sir Andrew Fraser. Still on, and enter a great building with several departments, where the whirr of the weaver is heard, and the noise of the loom. Here *cotton cloth, good tweeds, fine Tibetan rugs, and most beautiful carpets* are all being produced by the deft handling of men and women, boys and girls. Still pass on, and another department where *Tailors* are hard at work, some masters of the trade, others only learning. Still on, and a new building is entered, the memorial recently built, where *Carpentry*, *Carving*, and the *Blacksmith's art* are all being fostered and applied to good purpose. Nor is the limit yet reached. A good *Dye-house* has long been needed for giving the many fabrics the attractive hues that charm the eye; and on one afternoon of our stay Mrs Ogilvie had the pleasure of laying the corner memorial-stone of the 'Mrs Graham Memorial Dye-house.' When so doing she gave expression to the admiration so widely felt at home for this devoted life that has ended all too soon.

Is this not an amazing work? In all, about 1000 workers are employed, either at the central establishments or in the district. Boys and girls are thoroughly trained in the different industries for which they are suited, and almost all are industries that on a smaller scale can be carried on in the homes of the people. The ambition of those in charge is to see that some useful industry is being taught in every village school, and practised in wellnigh every crofter's home. In the year previous to our visit the sales amounted to one lakh of rupees—about £6500. And most of this has gone to enrich the people, to reward their industry, and to help forward an industrious, God-fearing folk. Yes, God-fearing; for every day in every branch of the industrial work instruction in the Christian religion is earnestly and lovingly imparted. Nor is general education neglected. It is here, to one or other of the industrial departments, that the pupils from the schools come daily for a little while; and to the schools the industrial folk go daily up for a little while also. Head and hand and heart are all looked after. Is it not right to say that the little seed has become a great tree?

IV. 'THE CHURCH' IN KALIMPONG.

And how about *The Church?* Two episodes of the week bore eloquent witness that with the Church it is well, and this whether we think of the Church in the narrower sense as the local congregation, or in the wider sense as the Body of Christ in the Eastern Himalayan Field.

We were exceptionally fortunate in the date of our visit. Sunday was Christmas Day, and with the Christmas Service there was combined a Harvest Thanksgiving Service, for it was the time of the harvest. Four local congregations joined their forces for the day, the parent congregation of Kalimpong and three country congregations from 'parishes' not far off. The beautiful church was filled, which means that over 400 worshippers were present, and the harvest gifts made rare adornment. Great stalks of sugar-cane formed an arch over the chancel, and decorations were on every side. But the most striking offerings came when along the aisle marched men and women laden with sacks of rice or maize or millet, which they emptied on the heaps that steadily

Church and Mission House, Kalimpong.

Mission Workers of Eastern Himalayas.

grew in front of the chancel. Vegetables in bundles and eggs in baskets were abundant. With gladness and purpose of heart do these people make offerings unto God.

It was all a glorious change since last we had worshipped in this church, eighteen years before. Then the church was seemly, now it is stately; then there was a fair congregation, now the church is thronged; then there was but little orderliness, now a reverent body of worshippers, conscious that they are in a House of God. To speak to this people from the pulpit was a moving experience; and when these simple hill-folk broke out into the old Christmas hymn of the Church universal, "O come, all ye faithful!" wonder, thanksgiving, exultant joy, and a great sure hope all combined to make an ecstasy of feeling. Truly here we walk by sight as well as by faith, for the Kingdom grows before one's very eyes.

Of the Church as an organisation, bodying forth Christ to the hill-people of the Kalimpong District, we had a delightful view on the previous Thursday. The *Presbytery of Kalimpong* was to meet. It numbers some twenty ministers and elders, but there had been invited that day other thirty teachers and catechists from far and near, and there were also the missionaries. The day opened with breakfast, as most days do; but not with breakfasts like this breakfast. The long verandah of the hospitable Mission House became a banqueting-hall. An extensive row of tables stretched from end to end, and no fewer than seventy men and women, Indians and Europeans, sat down together! It was splendid evidence of the cordial relations of the different racial elements in this happy land. On every side was frankness, friendliness, and geniality. Dr Graham, the father and host, beamed one long blessing on his guests all through the breakfast, a short but hearty word of welcome was spoken to the visitors from Scotland before we rose, and a reply was made of like kind. Then came the taking of the photograph by Mr Purdie, ever kind, which is reproduced in these Notes, and makes further description quite unnecessary. But it was a fine breakfast!

The Presbytery met in the side aisle of the church after a Communion service at which the Moderator, Lakshman Singh, Dr Graham, and I officiated. Everything was done with a reverent quietness and orderliness that would have won the approval of the most fastidious home critic. Then the Presbytery was constituted, the members sitting in front apart, and the teachers and catechists forming an attentive group behind. Mr Lakshman Singh, the Moderator, is a shrewd old man. With his wise wrinkled face, pleasant smile, and impressive spectacles, he looks very much like a comely old Scots minister of fifty years ago. The proceedings were in the vernacular, and followed the usual Presbytery methods. But when from time to time matters of special interest arose, I followed the debate with the kind help of Dr Graham. Two themes of general interest may be mentioned :—

One is the marked attention that was paid by the Presbytery to the *Temperance Question.* The mountain air, as in some quarters nearer home, seems conducive in some cases to a love of strong waters, and as these are easily prepared the love is not sufficiently curbed. Mr 'Pussyfoot' Johnson had been up here recently, and had made a deep impression. Unlike many cold-weather visitors, this wise American, throughout his Indian tour, eschewed politics and stuck to his own business. It was strange, however, in this far-off corner of India, to hear Nepali speakers referring to 'Pussyfoot' Johnson with familiar ease. So small has the world become!

The other matter dealt with was more delicate and right action more difficult. In the Eastern Himalayas, as in Britain, the war experiences have often brought *matrimonial tangles.* Enforced separations of husband and wife have led to not a few breaches of the marriage vow, and now the Presbytery has to bring things back to normal decency and order. The Presbytery, be it remembered, is not a Presbytery of the Church of Scotland, but of the Presbyterian Church in India, and so has power to display the workings of the Indian mind unchecked by too much deference to Scottish precedents. How this affects practical points is shown by a case that came up that day for consideration. A man (a returned soldier) and woman had been living as married people for several years. The man's legal wife, in his absence during the war, had gone right away—or rather 'wrong' away,—with another man. The irregular couple's general respectability was vouched for. They wanted to be married, and readmitted to the Church. Divorce is too expensive at present, otherwise it would be easy for the man to divorce his absconding wife. Steps are being taken to cheapen the process, but this has not yet been done. What would the Presbytery decide? It decided to readmit the offenders to the Church after a 'formal' marriage had been celebrated. In effect this is the Church recognising a marriage where the State (as yet) would not. It is not Scots Church law this, but it is the mind of these Indian presbyters; and one may hope that a modification of the Indian legal procedure may speedily make it unnecessary for any such questions to be discussed.

There were other matters of wider interest, where the Presbytery had no difficulty in deciding what to do —*e.g.*, the need of seeing to the fuller education of the Christian children—out of 1154 children of school-going age, half were stated to be not in attendance; the establishment of a fund for augmenting the scanty salaries of Indian workers; the forwarding a request to Government that Indian Christians should be allowed to join a unit of the Indian Auxiliary Force (for the checking of disloyal rioting, &c.); and the arranging of measures by which Himalayan Christians moving to Calcutta should be looked after by Christian ministers. All excellent resolutions, and evidences that the *Presbytery of Kalimpong* is alive.

The afternoon of that day saw an important meeting of the *Himalayan Mission Council*—the body that links together and controls all the component parts of the Kalimpong Mission Group. It is composed of the missionaries and four Indian 'consulting' members, one being the prudent Mr Lakshman Singh. The meeting lasted three hours, and we discussed with profit many things connected with the working of the Mission, but these are matters of detail that need not be mentioned here. Only it will be seen that the Kalimpong Mission is fully organised, and organised for further growth—a matter this last of much importance, for Kalimpong itself is about to grow mightily. A 'New Kalimpong' is already more than talked of. A great stretch of land on the slope of the hill fronting the Mission on the farther side of a little valley has been bought by the Government, to be sold in plots to purchasers, and ere long it is more than probable that extensions will begin such as may transform Kalimpong into a second Darjeeling. Good it is that our Mission is planted firm and safe, and that a body of earnest men and women are in control.

V.

A last word ere we say 'good-bye' to this great Mission. Work is the order of the day, but some lighter hours come to the missionaries when they relax. It would be a disaster if this were not so. European residents are few, but they are very friendly, and little social gatherings are held from time to time. And the very fact that the Mission is so big makes possible a degree of mutual fellowship not feasible at smaller stations. Several such happy gatherings we shared while there: one that stands out in memory was the dinner on Christmas Eve in the Mission House. Dr Graham and his daughter Isabel were host and hostess. The guests (the missionaries, four friends, and we two pilgrims) numbered twenty-three, and a happy Christmas Eve of the good old order was spent. Games and music made the hours pass, and with 'Auld Lang Syne,' 'God save the King,' and 'O come, all ye faithful!' the unforgettable evening ended. These three—song, anthem, hymn—expressed well the deepest loyalties of our hearts,—love for the old Homeland, loyalty to our good and gracious King, and glad devotion to the Lord of Christmastide, the destined Lord of India—the Lord Jesus Christ.

CHAPTER XIX.

KALIMPONG—ST ANDREW'S COLONIAL HOMES.

To the average Britisher in India the name 'Kalimpong' suggests only one thing, and that has absolutely nothing to do with the great missionary work we have been considering. To him 'Kalimpong' means the place where are situated the *St Andrew's Colonial Homes.* There may be a Scots Mission there, or there may not. He believes there is, now that you ask him. But that Dr

Graham's Colonial Homes are there he is quite sure. The Homes touch his heart, they win his commendation, and if he be a logical man they secure his contribution every year. It does not matter much whether this Britisher be Scots Church or English Church, or even a little nebulous as to his personal Church affinities. The Homes are the concern of all the Churches, they have the warm approval of all good men, so they have his approval too.

The Colonial Homes are the creation of the heart and mind and lifelong devotion of John Anderson Graham. He had not been a year in India before the cry of the little waifs and strays of the Eurasian community—as it was then termed—reached and wrung his heart,—pitiful derelicts of mixed Indian and British blood, or yet more pitiful little ones as purely British as any boy or girl in the High Street of Edinburgh or the back streets of London, but fated to grow up in the alien environment of the slums of an Indian city. What to do with these children, white and brown alike, and how best to fit them for the hard life that lies before them, are questions that have been growing in urgency for two hundred years in India—indeed, ever since the British occupation began. In the old old days unions between British men and Indian women, often in honourable marriage, but still oftener otherwise, had resulted in a large community of mixed blood. As the generations passed the community gained a standing and respectability of its own. In the days of the Mutiny its men did splendid service in the British cause: 'Neill's Lambs' or the Madras Fusiliers, Skinner's Horse, and some other regiments of 1857 fame were for the most part recruited from this 'Domiciled European Community.' In the great merchant-houses of Calcutta, Bombay, and Madras, the subordinate posts were long filled by the educated youth of this mixed race. In

St Andrew's Colonial Homes—School and Cottages.

St Andrew's Colonial Homes, Kalimpong.

the Government services the middle and lower grades were largely staffed from this source; and still in the mercantile world and in the Government departments the community has its honoured representatives. But on the whole the trend has been downwards. The rise of the educated Indian, with a more economic scale of living and often a greater capacity for work, has ousted the men of mixed blood; and once ousted, the strong 'family' loyalties of the Indian do not permit any return. So it is that life gets ever harder for these half-brothers of our own, the downward slope is increasingly trodden, and more and more difficult is it for those who are down to ascend again. For the community the English and Scottish Churches have done much. There is not a large city in India where institutions for their benefit are not to be found, specially noteworthy being the great 'Lawrence Orphan Asylums,' named after that noble soldier-philanthropist, Sir Henry Lawrence. But these do not touch very pointedly the lowest stratum of all—the bairns who are 'nobody's bairns,' who for want of a helping hand are foredoomed by their birth to misery, and who if left 'unsalved' grow up to make yet more difficult one of the most difficult social problems that face the British in India. "How to find a training-ground for the character, a stimulus to the self-respect, and a field for the honourable employment of the poorer European and Eurasian child in India, so as to make him not unworthy of the blood which flows in his veins, is one of the gravest problems that confront the philanthropist or statesman." So says Lord Curzon, and he says truly. The problem is not yet solved, perhaps never will be fully solved, but St Andrew's Colonial Homes come nearer to a solution than anything hitherto tried in India.

Dr Barnardo's Homes in England and the Quarrier Homes in Scotland suggested to Dr Graham the lines that have since been adopted. Up in the salubrious heights of Kalimpong, as he thought anxiously on this sad problem of the plains, he had a vision. He saw the tiny boys and girls rescued from the great cities, where they never have a chance, delivered from an environment that stunts the body and kills the soul, and brought in tens and hundreds to the hills round Kalimpong. He saw the long hill-slope that stretches to the north of the Mission given up to the invaders from the plains, the hillside dotted over with attractive cottages, and the lads and lasses occupying them in families of twenty. He saw Scottish and English women of good sense and loving hearts installed in these cottages, and 'mothering' the young folk, who in too many cases never had known what a mother's love can mean. The vision grew, and he saw for the communal life great buildings rising—a central school with many teachers, store-houses and barns, a hospital well equipped and staffed, and many other things besides. Then he told his vision to the world, the Anglo-Indian world that has suffered many things at the hands of writers who do not know it. That world of business men and Army men, Civil Service men, of merchants and their assistants, of planters and engineers, and men of every occupation that Europeans in India follow, when it saw the vision unfolded, beheld the glory of it; and to-day, largely by its gifts and its steady support, but aided also by a sympathetic and discerning Government, the vision to-day is sober and glorious fact. There on the hill-slope stand twenty cottages, a noble school with a great clock tower, and a beautiful hospital where sick children are nursed back to health. There, too, are the buildings needed for a training in industrial arts—carpentry and engineering for the boys, and for the girls laundry-work and cooking, domestic economy, and the art of the needle. And there, most important of all, are 600 boys and girls, having their bodies made strong, their souls kept pure, and their minds equipped by stores of knowledge and the acquisition of power for the work that waits them when they leave the school to face the world. Little wonder that the Kalimpong Homes, and the man who has made them, stand very high in the thoughts of Anglo-India.

Two afternoons did we give to visiting this wonderful garden-settlement upon the hillside. The first was on Friday, 23rd December, and the date will become a red-letter day in the annals of the Homes, for the central duty of that afternoon was to lay the foundation-stone of the fine *School Chapel* that is to be erected as a memorial to the late Mrs Graham. Her heart was in the Homes quite as much as in the Mission. If Dr Graham has been the father of this great family of 600, Mrs Graham was the loving mother. Four afternoons every week of her life at Kalimpong did she give to the Homes, visiting the cottages and mothering everybody. And when she died, by her own request her body was laid to rest in the little graveyard on the hill, alongside the little mounds where sleep the children gathered early to their rest. It was a happy choice to make the School Chapel her memorial, and it evoked widespread approval when it was made known. Contributions from India and from Britain came in freely, and a sum not far short of Rs. 100,000 was in hand. So the foundation-stone might well be laid. And it was laid that afternoon with a service of quiet simplicity. Round the site were ranged the boys and girls of the school; Mr Simpson, the tried head-master, and his staff of teachers; the numerous missionaries; not a few Indian friends who loved and mourned her who was gone; and, most touching group of all, Dr Graham and his two daughters, with hearts at once sore and lifted up. With solemn words of dedication and earnest prayer to God for the Chapel that was to arise, and for the generations who will worship there, the stone was laid. Then followed a brief address on what the Chapel would stand for in the School's life; and after a heartfelt tribute to the memory of Mrs Graham came the Doxology, and finally 'God save the King.' Brief, touching, memorable, made yet more impressive by the very beauty of the situation and the suggestive outlook. The Chapel will ever look down on the great Mission below, where she whose name it bears did her life-work; and the spirit of brotherhood between the races which Homes and Mission typify cannot but bear fruit in the lives of those who here are trained.

The following afternoon we came again, and went round the well-equipped school, and the equally well-equipped hospital; also several of the cottages where the 'families' were at home. It was the Christmas holiday season, and Christmas glee was everywhere. In one large cottage stood a great Christmas-tree, and to fifty delighted children Dr Graham and I handed down the presents. We had our reward, for we too and my fellow-pilgrim all had presents from the tree! One visit in particular stands out in the memory. It was the visit to the 'Babies' Cottage,' where thirty very tiny bairns were as happy as bairns could be, rosy-cheeked and full of glee. There, as in every cottage visited, Dr Graham was simply rushed at as soon as he appeared. Every child claimed at least a finger, and as the fingers would not 'go round,' they had to be grasped by relays of delighted little ones, who found in him their happiest playmate of the day.

It is a big financial task that has to be faced every year by Dr Graham and the various 'Colonial Homes Committees'—in Calcutta, Bombay, London, Glasgow, and Edinburgh, but more especially Calcutta. It lies outwith the Church of Scotland's official responsibilities. Her contribution has been the free grant from the be-

On the Teesta River.

Thanksgiving Sunday—Bringing Collection to Kalimpong Church.

ginning of the invaluable services of Dr Graham. But unofficially members of the Scottish Churches, both in India and in Britain, have taken their full share in supporting this splendid philanthropy, which benefits the neediest children of all the Churches. Over half the number in the Homes to-day are labelled 'Church of England,' as is to be expected, for in India, as in the Empire as a whole, England is the predominant partner. And English supporters of the Homes are as keen and as generous as Scottish. But the best that both English and Scots can do to help is needed. Nearly Rs. 200,000 (£13,000) is the present annual estimate of expenditure. This takes some raising, and in these hard times the task is harder than it used to be. Economies are the order of the day in the Homes, and the multiplication of cottages has for the present had to be stopped. But the work is too good for this to be more than a temporary 'going slow.' Above all, Calcutta believes in it, and what Calcutta believes in, Calcutta will keep going —and going strong.

One cause of anxiety has lately arisen through the changed political arrangements in India, by which educational policy and administration have passed largely into Indian hands. Institutions or enterprises which have the British note emphasised are not expecting to benefit by this change when the question of grants-in-aid is being considered, for things British are rather out of favour in these days. And that the 'British' note in the Homes has been strong, and will be strong, is undoubted. But that the Indian note is strong too is equally unquestioned. The boys and girls there trained, in the great majority of cases, will be citizens of India. Their training as good citizens is a matter that concerns India first and last, and this will no doubt be gladly kept in mind by all wise Indians.

"Our object," said Dr Graham at the last annual

meeting in Calcutta, "is not to create a little England or Scotland or Australia on the Himalayas. It is to take what we think the best methods from these lands, and to bring them to bear on the character of our boys and girls. We do not claim to have succeeded in realising all our dreams in connection with the Homes, but we do believe that many of the boys and girls of the domiciled community who come to Kalimpong are being made into strong useful citizens of India; and it is on this ground that we claim with confidence the help of Government, as well as the co-operation of European and Indian alike."

. . . .

It is sometimes asked, What is the secret of Dr Graham's magical power? I felt that the secret was revealed that afternoon at the 'Babies' Cottage.' He has the heart of a little child. By that he wins the children; and by that, when he goes to the big cities and speaks to wealthy merchants and mighty rulers, he wins the grown men too. There is no power on earth greater than that of the childlike heart, and it is his. Other powers as well he possesses in abundance; but this is what tells most. He speaks to men of Kalimpong and the Homes and the little children there; and the child-heart that he has kept unchanged through sixty years of strenuous life is revealed as he speaks. Men see it, and they are glad. They feel its magnetic power. All that is best and purest in themselves is stirred, and they willingly let themselves be led by this man with the heart of a little child, whom God has made the chief shepherd of the waifs and strays of Anglo-India.

On Monday midday, 26th December, we said a reluctant 'good-bye' to Kalimpong. Dr Graham had gone on ahead, as he was due at Allahabad, where we were to meet him later in the week; but Mr Purdie, ever kind, saw us comfortably despatched in two rickshaws—the only two in Kalimpong, for this mode of locomotion is here quite a recent experiment. But it proved a most successful one. Down the steep hillside the sturdy runners went, taking us through ever-changing scenery of wondrous beauty. Quickly the temperature changed, wraps were discarded, and by the time we reached the Teesta Bridge it was a genial sub-tropical atmosphere that enveloped us. Two miles along the side of the Teesta brought us to *Kalimpong Road Station*, the northern terminus of the Teesta Valley Railway. By this railway we were to journey to Siliguri, and we had been told by many of the feast of beauty we should have. They were right. The rail runs along the riverside all down the long gorge, and all the way we were looking out on a perfect panorama of beauty. Below rushed the opal-green river, fresh from the glaciers of the Himalayas; above the river rose the mountains sheer, clothed to the very summits with magnificent forest. It was a long succession of the Pass of Killiecrankie and the mountains round Pitlochry, but with everything on a scale that made our Scottish glories seem very miniature after all. The forest and jungle through which we passed were luxuriant with every variety of tropic growth and fantastic creepers. Here we knew lurked tiger and leopard and boar, but they did not trouble us. The darkness fell, and by 7.30 P.M., after a memorable run of three hours' duration, we reached Siliguri. There was an hour to wait before the Calcutta train would start; and as the Indian custom is, dinner was served in the refreshment-room. But something better than dinner—a warm Scottish welcome. Mr and Mrs Parker, a planter and his wife on an estate in the Terai, fourteen miles away, had heard that we were coming, and had motored in to see us and have a talk about Scotland! They were our hosts that evening, and as we talked and talked, I fear the glories of the Himalayas and the beauties of the Teesta were forgotten. Scotland dominated all. Our host was from Glasgow, our hostess from Campsie; we were from Aberdeen—and we all agreed that there are many things in Scotland that India cannot touch! And one of the best is that regard of the Scots for the Kirk, that drew to Siliguri that night these two strangers to greet us two strangers. As soon as we clasped hands we were none of us strangers, and when they sped us on our way to Calcutta we were four good friends.

CHAPTER XX.

ALLAHABAD—AN INDIAN GENERAL ASSEMBLY.

IN Calcutta on this second visit we were only birds of passage, though so comfortable was the temporary 'nest' kindly provided by two devoted Scots Kirk friends, Mr and Mrs M'Nair, that we would fain have rested quite a while. But Allahabad was calling, and we took wing again. Now Allahabad is a great city, and the capital of a great province; but what drew us there were just two things—the Scots Kirk, with its fine congregation of the Black Watch; and the General Assembly of the Presbyterian Church in India, which was meeting there on the last four days of December.

To many in Scotland the Scots Church in Allahabad for a number of years yet will be thought of as the scene of the Indian ministry of that fine old veteran, Dr James Williamson, who after twenty years as chaplain at Allahabad served the Church in Scotland for wellnigh other forty years as the beloved minister of the Dean

Parish in Edinburgh. His picture hangs on the wall of the vestry of his old Indian church which he never ceased to love. Mr Dodd was ministering there on our visit, and on the New Year Sunday morning he and I conducted service before an exceeding fine parade of the officers and men of the famous Highland regiment that there is stationed. It was a privilege to wish them 'A Good New Year' in the name of the Church at Home.

And now as to the General Assembly of the Presbyterian Church in India. What is this 'Presbyterian Church in India'? It is the ecclesiastical organisation to which the Indian congregations of our own Missions, which we had been visiting, owe allegiance. The whole of our Indian Christians in the Panjab, in Calcutta, and in the Eastern Himalayas are members of this Church. So are all the Christians of the United Free Church Missions who are north of the Deccan—those of Central India, Rajputana, Calcutta, and Bombay; so are the Christians of the American Presbyterian Mission in the United Provinces; so are those of the Irish Presbyterian Mission; and now, for the first time, so are the thousands of Christians of the Welsh Presbyterian Mission in Assam. It is a far-flung Church, about as scattered as would be a Church extending from Edinburgh to Venice, and Berlin to the Pyrenees. It has fifteen Presbyteries and four Synods, and represents a Christian community of nearly 150,000 people. With the exception of the American United Presbyterian Church in the Panjab, all the important Presbyterian Missions in the northern half of India are included in this Church. It is a young organisation, for this was but its eleventh Assembly, only it has to be noted that the Assembly meets but every second year. The great distances to be travelled naturally tell on the attendance; and it said a good deal for the loyal devotedness of ministers and elders that out of 100 elected members no fewer than 65 were present. Three-fifths of these were Indians and two-fifths Westerners, either European or American. The Church of Scotland Mission representatives present were Dr Graham, Mr Ogg, and Mr Lakshman Singh from the Eastern Himalayas; and from the Panjab Mr Scott, Mr Nicolson, Mr Mehtab Din, and Mr Patrick (an Indian elder).

When I left India seventeen years before, this General Assembly was in its infancy, and was being trained and developed largely by the European missionaries. Now one was keenly anxious to see how it had grown in the interval. Had it ceased to be very much a 'paper' organisation, as it almost necessarily was at the beginning, and had it now reached the full stature of a mature and weighty council of the Church? No questions in India to-day connected with the Indian Church are more important than questions of this kind. The answers given form the best clue as to the timeliness for the Indian Church becoming independent of European co-operation. Judging by what I saw at Allahabad, I should say that the time has not yet arrived for such a severance between East and West. The Assembly has very markedly developed since the early days, and has long ceased to be a 'paper' organisation. It is a reality, and has done incalculable service in bringing these many widely-scattered Presbyterian Mission Churches into a living unity. At this very meeting fresh advances in this direction were made. Indian members took a prominent part in the business. An Indian minister sat as Assembly Clerk. The Moderator's chair was occupied indeed by a well-beloved European, our own Dr Graham, but repeatedly it has been filled by an Indian, and this may be regarded as the common practice for future years. Still for some time yet the Church will best be served by a continuance of the happy cordial co-operation of the two races. Nothing could have been more beautiful than the relations between the two communities, whether the members were at work or at leisure. There was no colour bar—no bar of any kind. In that atmosphere of brotherliness the vexed question of Church and Mission scarce needed to be touched, and on more than one occasion the positive gain from the association of Indian with European and European with Indian was very apparent.

One such instance arose when by an Indian member the duty was urged of the Indian Presbyterian Church undertaking a *Foreign Mission* of its own. Such a Mission would do much to bind the scattered Presbyteries together, and would raise the spiritual life of the whole community. The idea caught the imagination of the Assembly at once. It had been mooted before, and when an overture from a Presbytery was tabled that *Tibet* should be chosen as the field and the work immediately begun, there was a storm of enthusiasm. At once there and then they would begin. Then it was that the calm judgment and riper experience of the Western members came in to put the Assembly on constitutional lines; and it was decided to approve the proposal, let a committee develop a scheme, and send it down to Presbyteries for consideration. No doubt it will go through at next Assembly, but then it will be a scheme well planned and with the backing of the Church behind it.

Church Union supplied another case of the enthusiasm of the East needing to be tempered by the experience of the West. A scheme of union with the Congregationalists was under discussion. Such a scheme has already been successfully adopted in South India, and will be here—but first let there be due constitutional examination of the scheme in all its bearings. So urged a prudent Western leader. "Oh, you Western brothers," cried an enthusiastic Indian, "it is you who are hindering

K

Church Union in India. Leave us to do it, and we'd have union everywhere to-morrow!" Very likely so they would; but what of the day after to-morrow? Their enthusiasm is magnificent, but not always wise. Not by defying history, or brushing aside constitutional practices which history has justified, will the cause of the Indian Church be best advanced. Here, as in other spheres of Indian life, the union of East and West had better continue. And if one may judge by the heartiness of the welcome given to the representative of the Western Church by these brethren of the East, *they* have no desire to see the bond of brotherhood weakened in the least degree.

The defects one noticed in the proceedings were almost all those of youth; and the merits of youth were just as noticeable. Idealism, courage, enterprise—they were all there; and what a gain to any Church are these! From the General Assemblies of the West this young sister of the East has undoubtedly still much to learn; but give her time and she will learn it all right.

And there are some points where the Assemblies of the West might with advantage sit at the feet of this young Assembly of the East. Have we nothing to learn from the notice issued to members summoning them to the Assembly? It gives on one page some practical counsels as regards the journeys, the trains, the accommodation, and other matters of the kind; and here are the opening and closing counsels:—

(1) Come to the Assembly with all the enthusiasm you possess.

(7) Get here before the opening hour on the first day, and don't plan to leave before the final Benediction is pronounced.

Good counsels these for the Assembly of any Church!

And as an example of the way to seek God's presence,

as well as to confer regarding His work, surely here is a fact worth recording. On the Sunday that closed the proceedings, from 7 A.M. until 3 P.M., the whole Assembly gave itself to devotion, unbroken by any interval for food. For eight hours communion, prayer, praise, meditation, exposition. By common testimony men felt they were on the Mount of God and with God. 'Never an Assembly have we had so good as this,' was their glowing pronouncement, and with the light of God shining upon them, they returned to their far-separated fields, strengthened for the work that lay before them. What has Scotland to say to this?

Back to Calcutta we went on the Monday, an eighteen-hours' run; there a halt for twenty-four hours with our kind entertainers, and on the evening of Tuesday, 3rd January, we were at Howrah Station, with the whole of the northern part of our pilgrimage behind us, and with faces set towards the farthest South. Mr Drummond Gordon, kind and thoughtful to the last, was there to see us off. Away into the darkness moved the train, and the second half of our Indian journeyings had begun. Ceylon was our objective. Had there been found a timely steamer we had gone by sea, but Ceylon had to be reached by the Sunday, and this meant the long train journey. On Thursday we reached Madras, tarried there for six hours, and then off once more by the South India Railway on a thirty-six hours' journey to Colombo. Past many towns of ancient fame: Trichinopoly, with its great rock; Madura, with its mighty temples; through many leagues of rice-fields; past hundreds of gleaming reservoirs well filled with water, for the monsoon was over; and at last we approached the toe of the great Indian Peninsula. Ceylon is the ball that fronts the toe, and between ball and toe at one point is 'Adam's Bridge,' a succession of marshy islets. Over these the railway now goes, thanks to good engineering, and brings us finally to the open sea. Twenty-two miles away is the north-west corner of Ceylon, and of the passage across those miles it is sufficient to say that is neither worse nor better than the passage from Dover to Calais. The names of the ports are a little more difficult—Dhanushkodi is that on the Indian side; Talaimanaar that on the Ceylon coast. A night journey in the train from Talaimanaar did the rest, and on Saturday morning, after four nights' and three days' travelling, we received at Colombo a welcome from Mr and Mrs Macmichael that all the Highlands could not beat for heartiness. The toil of the long journey found ample compensation.

CHAPTER XXI.

CEYLON—"WHERE EVERY PROSPECT PLEASES."

When Bishop Heber wrote what is still the most popular missionary hymn in the English language, he made a reference to Ceylon which has banned for ever that hymn from use by the churches of the island. The reference consists of two lines. The first line is gloriously true, and I quote it in the title of this chapter. The second line is not quotable. It suggests that the inhabitants of Ceylon have a double dose of original sin, which is a pure libel. I suspect the difficulty of finding a suitable word to rhyme with 'Isle' was allowed to deflect the bishop's judgment as to the character of the people who inhabit the isle. Anyhow my judgment, after nine days' residence and close contact with many of the men

Tooth of Buddha at Kandy, Ceylon.

On the Way to Kandy, Ceylon.

and women on whom 'Ceylon's spicy breezes' blow, is the very opposite of the bishop's. But, of course, it has to be kept in mind that these contacts were mainly with the congregations of the Scots kirks in Kandy and Colombo!

Of our nine days in that tropical paradise four were spent in Kandy and five in Colombo. These are the two chief centres of British life in the island, very different from each other, but both uncommonly attractive, and as spheres for the Church's work unusually interesting.

The train journey from Colombo to KANDY, which we made on the afternoon of the Saturday of our arrival, takes about four hours, and carries one through some of the loveliest scenery imaginable. It does not indeed compare in grandeur or variety with the journey to Darjeeling; for while Darjeeling is 7000 feet in height, Kandy is but 1600 feet. But for rich tropical vegetation, for softer mountain scenery, for 'thrills' experienced at many a sharp curve in the laborious ascent, for a succession of striking landscapes on emerging from the many tunnels that pierce the mountain-sides, the journey is hardly to be surpassed. And when at last Kandy is reached, you find yourself in a paradise of beauty that is unsurpassable. Round a lovely lake of three miles in circumference is an encircling ring of beautiful hills, which slope gently away to heights of 500 or 600 feet, all clad from base to summit in a luxuriant and varied robe of green. Bungalows of planters or other settlers, as well as those of prosperous burghers and Singhalese, are dotted at intervals on the hillsides, and stretching away from one side of the lake is the town of Kandy. In the middle of the town stands the Scots Kirk, conspicuous from afar by its shapely tower.

The kirk has stood there for well over sixty years, and has goodly memories behind it—memories of the great old days when Ceylon was a coffee-growing territory of world-wide repute, and Kandy was the centre of the richest coffee district in the island. Scotsmen abounded; so did wealth, and the Scots Kirk flourished exceedingly. Seven Scots ministers, Government chaplains mostly, were at work in seven centres, and all went well. Then came the coffee blight, which ruined for the time the planting industry; and on the back of that came the Disestablishment Act of 1881, which ended the supply of chaplains by Government, and the outlook was dark indeed. But still later came the great success of *Tea* in place of coffee, and the return of a fair measure of the old prosperity. And in time came too the adjustment by the churches to their new conditions, whereby local self-support and help from the Home base, through the Colonial Committee of our Church, have taken the place of the old Government provision. It has meant for a time restriction of the field of operations more than is desirable, but there are signs of better things.

Kandy Kirk exists to supply the spiritual needs of three communities—the Scots planters in the neighbourhood of Kandy, and a wide district around; the Scots, both men and women, in business in Kandy, whether heads or assistants; and the Burgher community, the descendants of the Dutch, who were there before we were, and are as staunch Presbyterians as any Scotland herself can show. From the beginning of the kirk's history these three sections have formed the congregation, never more prosperous than in the days long gone by, when the late Dr Sprott of North Berwick was the ardent young minister. The congregation, like many others, has had its ups and downs. For two years before my visit it had been ministerless, but, thanks chiefly to the grit and devotedness of the Session Clerk, a keen burgher, the services of *some* minister every Sunday had been secured, and the church had lived through.

A week before our arrival, Mr Neil from Newburn, in Fifeshire, had come out to pull things together, and to keep them together until a permanent minister could be sent from Scotland; and the Sunday services when we were there formed a happy inauguration. It was a fine congregation that met for evening service, to whom it was a pleasure to give the greeting from Home. Everybody was in good heart and hope, as also was I. Mr Neil is a wonderful man. He had only been a week in Kandy, and yet he knew half the congregation, the whole staff down to the humblest servant of the great Queen Hotel where he and we were living; and as for the surroundings of Kandy, no more efficient or kindlier guide could be desired than he proved himself to be. All this in a week! The kirk is in capable hands.

Life was not a rush in Kandy as it had been for the previous three months. We had time to take in the beauties of the place, and to appreciate the kindness of several of the kirk folk, notably Mr and Mrs Pyper, whose beautiful estate was a delight to visit, and in whose car we motored round the upper slopes of all the hills that circle around Kandy; and Mr Jonklass of the burgher community, a prominent lawyer and a trustee of the church, whose lovely bungalow on the lake-side and whose personal reminiscences of European travel will long abide in our memories. The famous College for the sons of Kandyan chiefs and others, identified with the name of the principal, was closed for holidays, but Mr Fraser kindly saw that we had a glimpse of its greatness. But there is something more famous in Kandy than either the kirk or the college. There is the *Sacred Tooth of Buddha*, the treasured relic guarded with the utmost care in the Buddhist temple by the lake-side. The temple we saw, and also the crude frescoes on the wall depicting the tortures of the Buddhist hell, whose hottest furnaces are reserved for those who steal from Buddhist priest or Buddhist temple. But the Tooth we did not see. On great occasions it is exposed to the gaze of adoring multitudes, but private views are given only to such visitors as H.R.H. the Prince of Wales. The Crown Prince of Germany, to give him his old title, desired to see it, but his desire was not granted. It is shown, however, here, in picture, to all who read this book. If one thing is quite certain, it is that no human jaw ever held that tooth, which is two inches long and one inch in thickness; yet this is the most sacred object in the world for some five hundred millions of the human race!

On Wednesday night, 11th January, we were back in COLOMBO, the happy guests of Mr and Mrs Macmichael in their delightful manse. A great city is Colombo, and yearly it grows greater. It is the Charing Cross of the Eastern Seas, where all the routes of ocean steamers meet. From China and Japan, from Australia and the Straits, from Cape Town and Mombasa, from every leading port in Europe, and from Eastern ports of America, come the gorgeous liners and the humble but essential 'tramps.' The aspect of the city is worthy of its importance. Banks, mercantile houses, great warehouses, and endless shops confront one; and here, as in the great Indian cities, the reign of the motor is mighty and undisputed. Needless to say, the Scots are here in becoming numbers, and happily the kirk is worthy of the Scots. Twenty years ago one could not say that. The kirk of those days was quite respectable, but not at all attractive, and the situation, in the heart of the business part of the city and remote from the residential area, did not conduce to a good attendance on Sundays. But Mr Dunn, who was then the minister, and his session saw their opportunity and took it. For business purposes the site was valuable, and it was sold for a good round sum. With this a suitable site was secured, a church was built which is a perfect gem, also a manse, which is the best in the East, and a fair balance was set aside as the nucleus of an endowment fund. Good business? Yes; but the purchasers of the old site did better. They built palatial premises on one half of the site, and sold the other half for more than they had paid for the original whole! So at least I was told. But the kirk did sufficiently well.

The Scots in Colombo are much given to hospitality, and the manse sets the fashion. Our five days there were marked by a succession of pleasant gatherings with our countrymen and countrywomen, who set themselves to show in this way how they appreciated the action of the Church in the Homeland in sending out two messengers and a message of remembrance. Specially memorable was an 'At Home' given by the session in the manse compound, and supervised by Mrs Macmichael and a company of ladies, when some eighty guests came along to meet us. Scottish most of them were, but by no means all, for the kirk has many friends outside itself, and numbers of these were there. It was all pleasantly significant of the place the kirk occupies in the thought of the European community of Colombo. Nor can one forget another happy episode, when along a beautiful road of twenty-two miles, through continuous groves of cocoa-nut palms, Mrs Walker motored us to Negombo—a 'country' seaside resort much favoured by the Colombo folk.

But Sunday was the chief day, and it gave the best evidence of how the kirk stands. At 9 A.M. we had a Communion Service, with ninety people present, all Europeans and mostly Scots; and in the evening the beautiful church was packed. It is not large—200 fill it comfortably, and 250 uncomfortably; but every detail in the arrangement of the building is perfect.

The memorial windows are a delight, and in exquisite harmony with the sacred purpose of the building; the music was the most finished we heard in all our tour; and the congregation was perhaps the most 'pucka' European of any of the Scottish congregations we had seen in the East. This last fact has an interesting explanation. In Colombo there are other four Presbyterian congregations, which belong to the Dutch Reformed Church; consequently many of the domiciled Presbyterian community, who in India would be a component part of the Scots Kirk congregations in the various cities, here have churches of their own. In Kandy it is not so; but in Colombo it is, and here the Scots Kirk is almost entirely a kirk for Scottish people. But what is best is this: they are people mostly who are proud of their kirk, to whom their minister and his wife are *friends*, and of whom accordingly the Mother Church at home may well be proud.

Let it not, however, be forgotten that the Mother Church of Presbyterianism in Ceylon is the Church of Holland, and not the Church of Scotland. The Dutch Reformed Church in Ceylon, the Burghers' Church as it is termed, has a long lineage, for it dates from 1658, when the sturdy Hollanders drove out the Portuguese from the island and reigned in their stead. Presbyterianism became the Established Church of the colony, fifteen ministers were maintained by the Government, State influence was used to win over the Singhalese to Christianity; and when in 1796 the island was ceded to the British, there were reported to be half a million Presbyterians in Ceylon. Alas! with the departure of the zealous State patrons of Presbyterianism the half million melted away. With the movement of most of the well-to-do Dutch to Holland or to Java the prestige of their Church decayed. Now for many years the

Church they left behind them has been entirely on its own resources. It has only seven congregations in the island, and of these five are in Colombo and the suburbs; but in Colombo its life is healthy and increasingly vigorous.

In 1882 these two small outposts of two great European Churches, the Scottish and the Dutch, decided to come together, and the *Presbytery of Ceylon* was formed. In reality it is of the nature of a Federation rather than a Union, and the functions of the 'Presbytery' are those of a joint Advisory Council. But it was a right thing to do, and the relations of the two sections of Presbyterianism are most brotherly.

One afternoon during our stay the Presbytery met in the Scots Church to greet the representative from the Church of Scotland, and a very interesting meeting we had. Mr Macmichael was in the chair, and spoke the cordial welcome; then three of the ministers of the Dutch Reformed Church gave informative addresses on the past and present of their Church. Particularly gladdening it was to learn that they had embarked on a definite bit of missionary work to the non-Christians of the island. But most interesting of all the contacts with our Dutch Reformed friends was a visit paid next day under the guidance of Mr Tweed, one of the ministers, to the fine old *Wolfendahl Church*, in the heart of 'old Colombo.' It is the best relic of the days of the Dutch occupation now extant—a great, somewhat gaunt, imposing building in the style of the old churches one sees in Rotterdam. There is the old 'Governor's Pew,' with the highly-ornamented chairs for himself and suite; there is the massive pulpit and the capacious pews, just as they were 150 years ago. Very massive, too, was the beautiful old silver communion plate, and quite new to me was the substitute for the flagons for the wine. It took the form of a magnificent embossed solid silver basin, not unlike a tureen. Into this the wine used to be poured from the bottles, and then ladled out into the Communion cups. Other times other ways. No doubt the Communion strengthened these old Dutch colonists just as much as it does us, though the wine be treated now in a somewhat different way.

A wholly charming island is Ceylon, and we were reluctant to leave it. But the appointed day drew on, and on the evening of Monday, 16th January, Mr and Mrs Macmichael saw us off, as we turned on our tracks and made for Madras. But theirs was not the last 'good-bye.' At a suburban station the train halted, and the son of my old class-fellow, Mr Dinwiddie of Ruthwell, came forward to the carriage, along with his wife, to load us with refreshing fruit, and to bid us a warm God-speed. It was a delicious memory to carry with us of the kindly Scots of Colombo, and their affectionate regard for the Kirk.

CHAPTER XXII.

MADRAS—CHIEF BASE OF INDIA'S CHURCH.

To all old Madrassis there is no place in India like Madras. So we two pilgrims felt when on the morning of Wednesday, 18th January, we reached the Egmore Station, and got a heartening welcome from Mr Mitchell, the devoted chaplain. We were 'Home' again! Far had we travelled and many cities had we seen, but none so good as this city. To Madras it was that, away back in 1885, we two had come to begin our work in India;

Madras Christian College.

and when in 1904 that work was finished, it was from Madras that we had sailed away. All our memories of those vanished years were good and gracious, and to be permitted now to revisit scenes so dear was an exceeding joy. Kipling, in his survey of the great cities of the Empire, pictures Madras as crooning to herself—

> "Clive kissed me on the mouth and eyes and brow,
> Wonderful kisses, so that I became
> Crowned above Queens!"

To those who know her best, crowned she still remains. Our many friends had made sure that a most gracious queen would she be to us. In the beautiful home of Mr and Mrs Turner we were surrounded with kindness all the time; the session of St Andrew's Kirk, our well-beloved, put a special car at our disposal—one which had been used by the Prince of Wales's suite the week preceding,—and missionary friends and Kirk friends were kind and hospitable to a degree. If the work to be done was strenuous—and it was—the environment was most enviable. But for the queenly car we could not have done half that was accomplished, for Madras is a city of vast distances, being forty square miles in area, but the car laughed at distances. Every day we were amazed to find how the new rapidity of transport had revolutionised things, and had made it possible to overtake duties in one day that in the old time would have occupied three. To tell here of the many things seen and done in the ten days of our visit it is necessary to group them in successive sections.

I.

There may be many who would hesitate to give Madras the primacy among Indian cities, but there are none who would not agree that the MADRAS KIRK is first of all the Scottish churches in the East. Built a hundred years ago by the East India Company at a happy moment when the leading officials of the Company in Madras were all keen Scots, there was no stinginess over the cost, and the result was a church which has been the joy and the pride of the Scottish community ever since, and will continue so to be. How much of the markedly prosperous record of the Scots congregation here has been owing to the existence of a stately House of God it is not easy to say; but it is quite certain that this contribution has been very great. It is a poor service to the cause of Scottish Presbyterianism in the East to be satisfied with an ignoble building.

Our greatest and gladdest surprise was the number of old friends who, after seventeen years, still were there to greet us. In any land an interval of that duration makes many changes in the personnel of a community, but in India the changes worked by time are exceptionally great. Transfers and retirals, as well as death, are continually making vacancies for new occupants to fill; and in Madras we found this to be the case—but far less than we had expected. A mercantile community, from which the kirk draws most of its members, is more stable than most. What we found in many cases was that the men and women whom we left in junior posts were now right at the top—older in years, but for the most part young as ever in spirit. One fact illustrates this. In the kirk-session we found eight elders: of these, all save one were members of the kirk congregation seventeen years before! This says much both for the salubrious climate of Madras and the even continuity of the Church's life; and when I add that two had been honoured with knighthood, Sir William Beardsell and Sir James Simpson, this tells its own tale as to the quality of the elders in Madras. Throughout our stay we were daily, and nightly, meeting old friends, but we met them in the mass on two occasions in particular.

One was at a large and very successful 'At Home' given by the kirk-session on the Saturday in the beautiful compound of the kirk. It was a perfect feast of old friendships. Often it was not easy to identify the smiling guests who did not need to 'speak' their welcome: it was so evident. Seventeen years make a difference in most people's outward aspect, yet there were few faces and fewer tones of voice which did not in a minute or two bid the long years go hence—and we stood to each other just as we had done long ago. There was much to learn as to what the years had brought, and, alas! as to what the years had taken. Later Mr Mitchell led us all into the spacious Church Hall, and there we had a concert, and of course speeches. Mr Mitchell's words were very kind, and it was evident that in their cordiality he spoke for all. What I said I cannot quite recall, but I know that to my wife and myself this afternoon moved the heart in many ways. Joy and gladness there was at meeting so many friends again, a sobering sense of the passing years, and a deep satisfaction that through all the years that had gone there had been here no forgetting of those old times which we had never forgotten—and never shall forget.

Sunday evening provided the other opportunity of meeting the people of the kirk as one united body. The kirk was filled with a fine congregation; Mr Mitchell led the devotions, Sir James Simpson read the lessons, and it was with strange feelings and mixed emotions that I entered the pulpit to preach the sermon. So much was familiar, so much was strange. But soon the strangeness vanished. On behalf of the Church at home I gave the greeting of affection, and then preached to the Scots of Madras just as I used to do twenty years ago. They are a fine people, these brothers and sisters of our own in India, and are worthy of the richest shepherding the Scottish Church can give them.

II.

The Madras Presidency has been the chief base on which India's Church has arisen, and it furnishes to-day the most visible proof that this Church is a great reality. Of the Christians in India two-thirds are located in the Southern Presidency. Madras *city* does not strikingly reflect this great preponderance as compared with the other cities in India. In no Indian city has the Christian Church yet obtained a very challenging publicity. In the country districts her greatest victories have been won, and this is conspicuously the case in the Southern Presidency. But Madras city, through its many Missions and its strong missionary institutions, has long exercised a great formative influence over the whole southern area. In these Missions, and also in the institutions, the Church of Scotland has its own share.

Our Women's Mission is our largest work, and to the centre of it all, the Mission House in the pleasant suburb of Kilpauk, our first visit in Madras was paid. Here, as often in past years, we blessed once more the foresight and the enterprise of her who thirty years ago acquired this fine property for the Mission—then Mrs Longhurst, now Mrs Ward,—living out her super-active life in quiet retirement on the Nilgiri Hills. A finer base for operations in Madras there could not be—an extensive compound, with ample space for every possible development, and in the centre a large and airy house, with good accommodation for the staff. This consists of five ladies, one of whom is always on furlough, and four are resident. Miss Graham was on furlough at the time of our visit; but from the ladies in the field—Miss Forbes, Miss Bain,

Miss Kelly, and Miss Evans—we received a true Madras welcome. The work of the Mission is twofold—that carried on within the Mission demesne, and that done in the great city outside. Within the compound is concentrated the work for Christian girls and women—a Boarding Establishment where 100 Christian girls are in residence; a fine school, where from Infant department to High School a sound Christian education is given; and the renowned Industrial School, where lace-making and embroidery are taught and practised with conspicuous success. Over the High School presides Miss Bain, and over the Industrial Department Miss Evans. The high encomiums passed on the work of these ladies by the Government Inspectors could hardly be bettered; and what we saw with our eyes and heard with our ears more than confirmed them.

First we visited the *Industrial School*—an extremely flourishing department. Every girl in the Boarding School comes here for part of the day, the daily routine being something like this: (*a*) clean and tidy their rooms, (*b*) Industrial School, (*c*) recreation for an hour, (*d*) school work. It is very fine work they turn out by their industry. To the Lace School, which was first established, the Embroidery School is a later addition, and true to the tendency of the hour *Indian* patterns and designs are increasingly in favour. This school is self-supporting; but more important than that is the fact that here every day 100 Christian girls and young women are being trained in an industry that will stand them in good stead all through life. The *High School* is overflowing its encasing boundaries, and is crying for more room—sure signs of efficient work. And it was very efficient work that we saw, though our visit was not well-timed. It was the opening day after the holidays, when the girls were 'finding themselves' again. All the classes were very interesting, but specially were we impressed with the quiet cultured demeanour of the older girls, their excellent knowledge of English, and altogether with the great developments in girls' education, since we knew it seventeen years ago. It is indeed a New India for the women as well as for the men. But we were to see more of this development later.

The *City Schools* are Miss Forbes's special domain, and verily, by her long years of devoted work, she has made them a sight worth seeing. Herself a thorough teacher, she knows how to impart thoroughness to the work of others under her. To four excellent schools she guided us—two in the neighbouring district of Pursewaukum, one in the great Mohammedan district of Triplicane, and the last and greatest in the heart of the city itself, the division known now as George Town (in honour of the visit of our gracious King). Everywhere there was the same glad sight of bright and happy Indian girls, keen in letting their accomplishments be seen, and if possible keener still in the exuberance of their welcome. The school is to them a place of light and life and happiness, and they knew that somehow the visitors who had come represented the friends far away, to whom their school was due. At all the schools the routine work was naturally very much the same—Bible lesson and repetitions, reading, writing, geography, singing, drawing, modelling, nature study, sewing, darning, and drill. Save for the first item, all are prescribed by the Government. But at each school there was some distinctive touch,—at one the girls gave a small play, 'The Shepherd Boy,' in English, with great zest and effect; in another they sang an ode of welcome specially composed; in a third—the fine school at Triplicane, which could be filled twice over to-morrow if we had a good building of our own—we found in the small courtyard a large clay model of India, 10 feet by 6, with the rivers and the mountains all accurately represented, the model being the work of the enthusiastic head-master. But perhaps most impressive of all was the George Town School—the crown of our City School work. In this three-storey building, the property of the Mission, in the very centre of a good class Indian population, 600 Indian girls were at work, happy as the day is long, delighted with their school and their teachers, and most warm in their welcome. At the entrance we were garlanded—a shower of rose-leaves fell upon us from the hands of a smiling band of Brahman girls, and an ode of welcome was recited. Then round the classes we went, and everywhere found efficiency and gladness. This is the largest Girls' School of its grade in Madras, and I believe in the Presidency also; and draws the largest Government grant for its work. Truly Miss Forbes is to be congratulated on the fruit of her busy years, and so too is Mr Daniel, the excellent Christian head-master of this school, and the indispensable lieutenant of the ladies in all the 'accounting' of the Mission. Later, Miss Kelly took us to still another school in Egmore village, where like activity was in evidence. In all about 1500 Indian girls are under instruction! And what does it all amount to, does any one ask? I answer this: Into these 1500 lives there comes a brightness such as they would not have known but for these schools. Into their minds comes the knowledge of a God who is their Father, who loves them each and all, and to whom they can ever turn. Into their hearts comes a love for those who bring such love to them, and in many cases too a love for this Jesus, of whose love their teachers are ever telling them. And when these girls leave the school and become themselves mothers of homes, the old influences abide, and little by little the spirit of Jesus works its own miracle in the men and women who make the homes of this New India that has come.

III.

On the Sunday morning at 8.30 we were at the *St Andrew's* (*Tamil*) *Church* in the Chulai district of Madras, a part of the city much favoured by the Indian Christians. It is a pretty little Church, and with its fairly large compound thickly planted with palm-trees makes a very pleasing spot in the centre of a busy quarter of the city. Some 350 of a community form the congregation, and there was an excellent representation that day. All were in their 'Sunday best,' and it is a very graceful and becoming best: in no case more so than in the fourscore maidens in white from our Mission Boarding School. Mr Silver, the overburdened but ceaselessly active missionary in charge of our Madras area, had come in from Arkonam for the day, and he and Mr Vethanayagam, the minister, conducted the service. Thereafter the kirk-session read an address reviewing the history of the church, and expressing their grateful affection for the Mother Church in Scotland, and to this I had peculiar pleasure in replying, for this church and people had been known to me of old. Not a people dowered with many rupees, for many of them are servants in European homes; others are clerks in offices on meagre pay. And not perhaps doing even what they could do in the direction of self-support; but they are getting on that way, and one remembers that times are hard to-day in India for humble folk just as they are at home, and makes allowances. But it touches one to note how proud they are of the old Scottish connection. Indians of to-day as they are, with all that that connotes of nationalist fervour, these men and women have no wish to cut themselves adrift from the mother that bare them. Man after man came up at the end, ay, and woman after woman as well, to speak a word concerning those who are long gone, and to shake the hands of him and her whom the Church across the seas had sent that day to visit them. They were not forgotten, and that gave them much happiness of heart.

In the carefully-prepared address there was one thing recorded that is worth telling here. One often hears it said that the European residents in India care but little for Missions. Of the majority this is unfortunately true. They care little and they know less, and the opinions of such on Missions, whether written or spoken, are worth simply nothing at all. But there is a large minority who both care and know, and who, when the needs of Mission congregations are put before them, are very ready with their help. In Calcutta we had already seen this, as has been told. And now in Madras this record of old-time doings showed the Scots Kirk congregation to have been, through the long years of its infancy, a nursing-mother to the congregation of the Tamil church. It was in the chancel of the kirk, back in 1851, that this congregation habitually met for worship; when in 1880 their own church was built the help of the Scottish congregation was freely given; down through the years the link between the two has never been broken; and in the year just closed (1921), from St Andrew's Kirk had come to help in the repairing of the Chulai Kirk and for the aid of the Mission at Arkonam no less than £175! I commend this fact to the consideration of any who may be inclined to believe that the Scots in India don't believe in Missions. The Scots who know what Missions really are, and what they mean for India, *do* believe in Missions, and they prove it by their gifts.

IV.

At 8 o'clock in the morning of the day before we left Madras the Advisory Board of the Women's Mission met in the Mission House, and together we discussed several important things that concerned the present and the future of the Mission. For the most part they had to do with financial or administrative details that have no place in this record. There was, however, one point of peculiar interest which may well be mentioned here. It touched the question of providing suitable means of locomotion for the missionaries. For their work some means of the kind is a simple necessity. Walking is out of the question in a tropical climate. If you wish to go anywhere beyond your own compound you must ride or drive or cycle. If you have to be out in the middle of the day in all weathers, as these ladies have to be, to drive in a covered carriage is the only possibility. Hitherto this has been the method. Very modest carriages have been provided, and still more 'modest' horses. But now horses cannot be got save for an exorbitant sum. The advent of motors has killed the old trade with Australia for horse-flesh; and if a ragged-looking steed is picked up from any source, the keep of horse and driver has now soared aloft to a degree not previously dreamt of. And besides this, now that motors are everywhere, all the life and work of the place is planned on a motor basis. The Advisory Board had no doubt as to what must be done. Horse and carriage and driver and syce and grass-cutter all must go, and for the Mission two Ford cars must be provided. Indeed, one had already been supplied, but another was needed. The cost was carefully gone into, and it was found that the keep of the two cars and drivers would not exceed that of the establishment required for the Mission carriages. So the recommendation went home, and will no doubt be favourably considered. For the need is not confined to Madras, it is felt to-day in every field. In the Panjab, in Calcutta, in Poona we found it just the same. In the Himalayan Field motors can't run, so there was no demand there!

But everywhere else the need is manifest. The extra cost involved is really the initial extra cost as between a Ford motor and a moderately good horse and carriage. How is this cost to be met? Here is how it is met in the American United Presbyterian Mission in the Panjab. There are twenty-eight stations there, and each station has a motor! Given by the Home Committee? No, not at all. Presented by individual donors in America, and the *upkeep* undertaken by the Home Committee. Will Scotland follow suit?

But mark this Advisory Board before we leave it. Who constitute it? The missionaries, the chaplains, and several of the leading members of the Madras European mercantile community, who are also members of the Kirk, such as Sir William Beardsell, one of the most successful merchants; Sir James Simpson, chief partner in a leading firm; Mr William Hutton, chief engineer to the Government; and Mr William Lamb, acting-manager of the Madras branch of the Imperial Bank of India. How is this for the interest of European business men in Missions? And this is a sample of what is to be found all over India. Wherever you have laymen with whom Religion counts, you find active, willing, and helpful friends of Christian Missions.

CHAPTER XXIII.

MADRAS—WHERE UNION IS STRENGTH.

ONE of the chief lessons learned by the Churches from the World Missionary Conference, which met in Edinburgh in 1910, was the necessity, as well as the duty, of co-operating in the Mission Field. It was a lesson that had been learned and practised in Madras for more than thirty years before the great Conference met; and though co-operation is now the policy adopted in well-nigh every field where Christian Missions find themselves in geographical contiguity, Madras remains the scene of co-operation's greatest developments, and supplies the two most convincing object-lessons in all India of its success. These are *The Madras Christian College* and *The Women's Christian College, Madras.* No hours of our Madras visit have left more impressive memories than those spent in these two colleges.

I.

The MADRAS CHRISTIAN COLLEGE is the life-work of one of the greatest missionaries Scotland ever sent to India—William Miller. It was in 1862 that he landed in Madras to take charge of the school or institution of the Free Church of Scotland, then at the very lowest point in its history. Since then its course has been steadily and strikingly upward and onward. Within ten years it had become the premier college in Madras, but the increasing demands in connection with higher education had by that time reached a stage when no single Mission could adequately supply them. If missionary education was to retain its place in the general educational system of the country, there had to be a linking up of the missionary forces for this common end. On his own Church and on other Churches concerned, Mr Miller urged this policy, and it was adopted. In 1877 the Church Missionary Society of the Church of England and the Wesleyan Missionary Society joined forces with the Scottish Free Church, and the *Madras Christian College* came into being. Later, in 1911, the Church of Scotland merged its own college in this united enterprise. In 1913 the London Missionary Society and the American Baptist Missionary Society were added to the number of 'Contributing Bodies,' and in this present year, 1922, still another body has entered this missionary 'combine'—the Reformed Church in North America. Seven Churches, representing Scotland, England, and America, all banded together to support this great Christian educational effort in South India! It is a convincing demonstration to non-Christian India of the essential oneness of Christian Missions, and it has made possible an enterprise of the utmost value in strengthening the Christian influence in India to-day. Over 800 students, who hail from all parts of Southern India, throng the class-rooms of the college, and 900 boys are on the roll of the Collegiate School. Under the principalship of Dr Macphail there is at work a staff of twelve missionary professors drawn from Scotland, England, and America, and a band of seventeen Indian lecturers. The missionaries are representative of the various Churches co-operating, the Church of Scotland having normally two on the staff, but at present only one, albeit a very worthy one, the Rev. A. J. Mackenzie. Away in far-off Scotland lives the "Honorary Principal," the Rev. William Miller, D.D., LL.D., C.I.E., now over fourscore, with his bodily vision sadly impaired and his physical strength much diminished by the passage of the years, but with heart still fixed on that beloved College wherewith he has dowered Southern India, and with mind still active in planning measures for its yet greater good.

"Will you come and visit the college on Monday, and address the Christian students?" So my old and valued friend, Mr Meston, the Acting-Principal, had asked; and gladly, on 23rd January, the visit was paid. I had known the college intimately in my old Madras days, for I had sat for years on the College Council, and was eager to see how things had changed during these last seventeen years. The greatest change of all was the sight in the hall where the Christian students assembled. I expected about 50: there were 200. The Christian students now number about 25 per cent of the total. They form now so appreciable an element in the life of the college that the name of the college has got a new connotation; and the old gibe about the Christian College being a college where there were no Christians has gone quite out of date. That every fourth student in this great college should be a Christian, instead of every tenth or twelfth as used to be the case, is significant evidence as to the general progress of the Christian community and the Christian Church in these intervening years. Once every month, at the regular Bible hour, the Christian students are thus gathered together, and their sense of solidarity and responsibility gets added emphasis. It was a rich pleasure to speak to them that day on the special contribution it falls to them to make to the developing spiritual life of India.

Then came the round of the numerous classes, where everything was going on as it ought to do, and where the ready welcome given by these sons of the East to a friend from the West was particularly gladdening. Buildings, equipment, classes, staff, all had grown greatly since I knew them last; indeed, one felt that further growth in the buildings and equipment had now become a pressing question, very difficult of solution, because the college, great in extent although the buildings are, is now engulfed in the sea of warehouses and offices which surround it on every side. Other colleges similarly situated in this city area are having to face the prospect of an escape to the suburbs, and this same question will also confront the Madras Christian College at no distant date. One might write much on the many-sided life of the students as now catered for by the

Two Indian Lecturers in Women's
Christian College, Madras.

Women's Christian College, Madras.

college—their hostels, their societies, their sports,—but it is enough to say that as I found in Calcutta so did I find in Madras. The college is content with nothing short of rendering the best service possible to the body, mind, and spirit of every student within its walls.

The cost of an institution like this is great, and grows greater in these times of economic difficulty. Two lakhs of rupees represent the annual expenditure. Half of this comes from the fees of the students, a quarter from Government grants, and a quarter from the contributions of the Home Churches. But its value to India is not to be estimated in rupees. Two facts connected with its life supply a better index to its worth. One is the extraordinary love for the college that dwells in the hearts of those who have been its students. What the Universities of Oxford and Cambridge, what those of Edinburgh or Aberdeen, are to their alumni, that the Madras Christian College is to its old students. Every year they hold their 'College Day,' when former students, many holding high positions throughout the Presidency, flock to Madras to keep the feast of their *Alma Mater*. Then they testify anew to the reverent and loving admiration they have for their now aged chief, and plan how best they can help the beloved college which has made them what they are.

But more eloquent even than these tributes is the admitted power and influence which these 'Christian College Men' are exercising in the many centres where they have found their life's vocation. The high ideals of life and duty implanted in them when students in very many instances affect for good the whole of their later public life. And never was this more true or more valuable than to-day. In the Legislative Council of the Madras Presidency twenty of the members are old Christian College students, so is one of the Indian Cabinet Ministers, and so are all the Under-Secretaries of the

Government. What this means for the developing life of the State was shown in November 1921, when a debate took place in the Legislative Council on the proposal to introduce a 'Conscience Clause' in all educational institutions aided by Government. By this, attendance at the 'Bible Hour' would have been made entirely optional, and very soon outside influences would have made it general. The proposed measure would have paralysed the college in its main religious aim. But in the debate member after member arose, told out what he owed to the Christian College, declared frankly that only the missionaries had brought education to high-caste and non-caste alike, and stated that to pass such a measure as was proposed would be both a hurt and a shame to India. The proposal was thrown out by 61 votes to 13—the best tribute to missionary education that has been given in India for many a day.

II.

A large part of Madras is a veritable Garden City. This is the wide-encircling suburban ring, where spacious dwellings of European residents or of Indian gentlemen abound, each surrounded by its own great 'compound' or grounds. In the best part of this Garden City, within a beautiful compound of eleven acres, stands the WOMEN'S CHRISTIAN COLLEGE. It is a very modern institution compared with the men's college, for it dates only from 1915. It had no day of small things: it came into life full grown—at least sufficiently so to take its place at once as one of the leading colleges in India. It owed its origin to developments in women's education in India, and especially in South India, that simply compelled the evolution of a Women's Christian College. Every Mission had its Girls' Schools, and from many of these specially bright pupils were passing out, eager to go further, but further they could not go. For the University Course there were only colleges for men; and while here and there a daring woman student might be found who claimed and received admission to these, it was not a practice that would ever commend itself to India. Then too some of the professions were calling loudly for qualified women—notably the teaching and the medical professions,—women of culture and capacity, and in sympathy with modern life. So it came about that the many Missions at work in South India took counsel together, with the Rev. Dr Pittendrigh as chief mover, and as the result of the counselling, and of the cordial co-operating of the Home Churches in Britain and America, this Christian College for Women became an accomplished fact. Twelve Churches or Societies combine in this truly great enterprise. Of these, six are British—the Church Missionary Society, Church of England Zenana Mission, London Missionary Society, Wesleyan Missionary Society, Church of Scotland, and United Free Church of Scotland. The other six are Transatlantic—American Baptist Mission, American Madura Mission, Methodist Episcopal Mission, Canadian Presbyterian Mission, American Arcot Mission, and American Lutheran Mission. A difficult team for united work? So some might think, but it has proved one of the most efficient and harmonious teams which has ever existed in connection with inter-Church activities. In the Field this is no surprise, for there sectarianism dies; and that where *Missions* are concerned it has largely died at Home as well, is proved by the complete success which has marked the co-operation of these twelve bodies, American and British, working through two Home Boards, one on each side of the Atlantic. There has never been anything but perfect brotherly harmony —or I should perhaps say 'sisterly'—from the very beginning. Happily, the lady chosen as the first principal, Miss Eleanor M'Dougall, has proved a perfect choice. Alike by nature and by grace she is supremely qualified for guiding the life of a college with so very diverse an ecclesiastical parentage. Among the staff this diversity is reproduced, as it also is among the students. Yet the note of unity is as supreme and overmastering in the life of the college as it is in the councils and actions of the controlling Boards.

Friday, 20th January, was the day of our visit to the college—an unforgettable day! It began early. By 8.30 A.M. we were driving up the fine approach that winds through the extensive compound, with its many trees and fine expanse of grassy sward—and then the stately building. We had known it of old, when it was the lordly residence of one of the highest in the Madras Civil Service, and the centre of much hospitality. Now it houses a much larger family, and serves a yet higher end. Save for an 'airy' dormitory on the roof, and the great dining-hall on the ground floor, the many rooms of the building have been transformed into excellent class-rooms. Near at hand rises the splendid new three-storied hostel which houses eight professors and some seventy students; and there are other buildings besides, where are the chapel, the sick-room, and additional hostel accommodation. Altogether a fine and impressive equipment seen only from the outside. Miss M'Dougall, who met us with a very warm welcome, was now to show us that the inside was equally fine and impressive. But first she called us to an outside view. Under the shady trees detachments of the students were at drill. One did not know whether to admire more the tall lithe figures of the students and their alert graceful movements, or the vigour and precision of the American lady who was drilling. Clearly, however, the cult of the physical is not forgotten. Going inside we were then introduced to the staff—a delightful octette of cultured, capable, purposeful Christian ladies, all in love with their work, with their students, and with their surroundings. Little wonder, I thought, that with such a staff and such a head the college should be the admired of all.

Introductions over, we went to the college chapel—a good-sized hall set apart for the purpose of worship alone. Soon it is hoped that a chapel specially built will arise; indeed, since returning home, I have heard of a gift of $10,000, but in the meantime this suffices. Worship is no perfunctory duty here. It is a hallowing of the day and of the day's work. The whole college assembled, 130 young Indian women-students, and Miss M'Dougall, following the daily custom, conducted the service. It was brief, but singularly impressive. First, a Scripture sentence of Invocation, then five minutes' silent meditation and prayer, followed by a lesson, and two or three short suitable prayers—for the college, for former students, for old friends, for the peace of India, for grace and power to serve their day and generation,—all closing with a hymn. Before the hymn, on this special occasion I was asked to address the students. It was a privilege that will remain unique in my experience, and was greatly prized. I felt that I looked on one of the fairest scenes all India could show—130 of her Christian daughters, cultured and full of faith, keenly alive to the new era that has opened in their country's life, and all desirous of making their contribution thereto. Many congregations I had addressed in India that had moved me exceedingly, but none more than this which gathered that morning in the chapel of the Women's Christian College.

From the chapel Miss M'Dougall and Miss Stevens led us round the buildings. All was delightful, and especially so the admirable hostel arrangements. A study-bedroom for each student is the rule, but there are also larger rooms where three, four, or five students are grouped. The classes were next visited, and one's admiration rose ever higher with the deepening sense of the thoroughness of the teaching, the eagerness alike of professors and students, the quiet beautiful orderliness, and the rich cultured Christian tone of the whole college. Nor is it in the classes only that training for life is given. The college has its different Societies—Literary, Debating, Musical, Dramatic, Games, &c.—all of which are in charge of college committees, and which help greatly to develop the sense of responsibility and practical capacity among the students.

Following the round of the classes came breakfast in the large dining-hall. At the head table sat the principal and staff, and this day the guests. The students were at the many other tables which filled the hall. Nothing was formal at this meal, but everything spoke of the happy freedom of a big family. When dinner comes along there is, I understand, a little useful attention given to what is 'good form,' and at the head of each table there sits one of the staff. It is, indeed, a Home on a large scale, and when one remembers the widely contrasted areas and communities from which the students come, the marvel at the Home's success is multiplied. Happy are those Indian maidens who here are trained, and fortunate the country whose life they go forth to enrich.

For four years the curriculum lasts, culminating in the B.A. examination of the Madras University. Marked success at the examinations, and honours not a few, have been the experience of the college during its short existence. Over forty graduates have already gone out from its attractive hall. Most of these have entered the teaching profession, and others have found their sphere within the home in private life; but whether in the public or the private sphere, the old students are fast winning for the Women's Christian College the same great name as has for long been secured for the older college by its *alumni*. When we said good-bye to the principal the staff and the students, and drove away, it was with the feeling that we had seen one of the noblest sights in New India, and had looked upon one of the most valued contributions to India's progress which the Christian Church to-day is making.

III.

Madras city and district has long been the centre of a vigorous and successful Mission of the United Free Church of Scotland. This is quite distinct from the co-operative work in the two colleges in which the United Free Church has played a prominent part, and it was a very real pleasure to be able to see not a little of this distinctive work of our sister Church.

The *Women's Work* centres at Royapuram, the extreme northern extremity of Madras, and some six miles distant from the Women's Work of the Church of Scotland. There is therefore no overlapping, and when Union comes there will be no necessity for closing down any of the present activities. At Royapuram the two chief sights are the *Boarding School for Girls* and the *Hospital*. Both are truly great. The Boarding School and the Teachers' Training Institution make a fine combination. Over 200 boarders are in residence, Christian girls all. An imposing range of buildings contains many beautiful class-rooms, all equipped in the most up-to-date manner; and above the class-rooms are spacious dormitories. Of this far-famed work Miss Stephen laid the foundation nearly forty years ago, Miss Smart built upon it, and now Miss Greenfield and Miss Sage are developing it in accordance with the ideas of the new time. But the earlier builders are not forgotten. In commemoration of their great work and long service Indian friends have built a commodious 'Worship Hall,' which is really the chapel of the school. Not in all India had we seen quite so impressive provision for the education of large numbers of Christian girls as here.

From the school we went to the *Rainy Hospital*, a fine memorial of the late Miss Rainy, and here again one has to say that among the Women's Mission Hospitals in India we had not seen the 'marrow' of it, for the generous scale of the buildings and the ample provision of medical equipment and staff. Dr M'Neill and Dr Alexander took us round the wards, and everywhere there were the same happy Christian tone and signs of high efficiency. A new Dispensary was 'opened' on the day of our visit, when Dr M'Neill made an interesting introductory statement, and I had the privilege of declaring the building open, and of dedicating it with prayer.

Earlier in the day we had seen the *Girls' High School* in George Town, a fine structure, where 400 Indian girls are daily in attendance. Altogether it is a big work for the girls and women of Madras that our two Scottish Churches are doing, and it was a joy to see it.

Twenty-five miles south-west from Madras lies Melrosapuram, in the area of the life-work of the late Rev. Adam Andrew. Mr Andrew was a pioneer in giving practical agricultural training to the outcastes. Over twenty years ago he founded here a little settlement of Christian converts, got jungle-land from Government, reclaimed it, started the humble folk on an independent life—in short, did on a smaller scale what we had seen going on at Youngsonabad. Gifts from Scotland helped him through the difficult years, especially gifts from

Mrs Melrose of Edinburgh, whose name was given to the settlement.

Now a further stage in the colony's progress has come. 'Vocational training' is the order of the day (would that a more modest word could be found for what must long be in most cases a modest enterprise !), and Mr Sutherland, who has succeeded Mr Andrew and shares his predecessor's zeal, at a cost of Rs. 18,000 has provided new school buildings, a hostel, and other things needed for a practical training in agriculture, and with thirty-five pupils the good work goes on another stage. Thursday, 26th January, was fixed for the opening of the new buildings, and Sir William Beardsell drove us out in his Rolls-Royce car to the spot. A large gathering of missionary and other friends were there, Mr Stewart in the chair. To me it was given to open the hostel, to my wife to open the school ; and with prayer to God, and universal good wishes, the new era at Melrosapuram began. Only a few months before had I stood at the open grave in Edinburgh where Mr Andrew had been laid to rest. In due time no doubt a stone will be erected to tell men who lies buried there, but Melrosapuram is a still better memorial—the memorial of one of the most devoted missionaries Scotland has given to India.

Conjeeveram, the third United Free Church station that we visited, lies between Melrosapuram and Arkonam. Away back in the pre-Disruption days Conjeeveram was a Church of Scotland station, for in 1839 John Anderson, the first missionary of the Church to Madras, opened here a school. In 1843 this passed to the Free Church, and ever since the station has been occupied. It was and is a post that calls for great courage and great faith ; for Conjeeveram is the 'Benares of South India,' the strong citadel of Hinduism, the site of some of the most lordly temples in all India. Preaching, teaching, and healing are the three well-proved methods followed by the Mission, and the centres of the latter two were visited by us—good centres both. The High School is a fine building, where 600 Indian boys are educated. It was the annual Prize Day, and the spacious hall was packed with the boys, and with many of the leading Indian gentlemen of the town. A speech by one pilgrim and distribution of the prizes by the other gave much pleasure to the two, and I think some pleasure also to the many. Next day we visited the well-conducted hospital, where Dr Macphail exercises her beneficent rule, and also the church which was being built just *outside* the municipal limits! No Christian church may yet be built inside this holy place.

In the morning our very kind host, Mr Maclean, took us to see the temples. Imposing and impressive they are, but oppressive too in the over-abundance of the sculptures—most of it to a Western eye being very *bizarre*, and not a little of it offensive. The sculptor's art runs riot alike in the grotesqueness of the workmanship and in its super-abundance. Yet all the same one remembered that here for nigh two thousand years had centred the religious devotion of untold millions of men, and that here still millions of our fellow-men find their holiest sanctuary. Walking round the vast enclosure and noting the impressive architecture, one realised the vastness of the task that Missions have taken in hand. And the eye fell on little scenes that added to the sense of difficulty. In one corner of the extensive enclosure two poor women were going round and round a little swelling on the ground, and offering at intervals small libations. They were worshipping a snake that was underneath! A worship born of deadly fear.

Again we heard the rapid tinkle of a bell, and the sound of music. Looking in the direction whence it came, we saw a Hindu runner carrying aloft a silver goblet. It was filled with water drawn from a holy well some miles away, and was now being borne to the great idol within! Still again on one side we confronted a temple of less embellishment than most, and we were told, "This is the temple of the great teacher Ramanuja, who perhaps comes nearest to the Christian ideals of any teacher Hinduism has had!"

Such is Hinduism—all things to all men, offering to each man what suits him best,—snake-worship to one, idolatry to another, high philosophy to a third. In this strange contradictory catholicity lies its greatest power.

IV.

Conjeeveram stands for 'Old India,' the India dominated by the Temple. In striking contrast to this was a view of the 'Newest India' which we got two days before we left Madras—that 'INDUSTRIAL INDIA' which in the great cities is coming ever more to the front. "Come out with me on Wednesday morning and see the Buckingham Mills," said our good friend and host Mr Turner one day. Promptly we accepted, for this was a side of India which we should not otherwise see at all. The Buckingham Mills and the Carnatic Mills, both under one company, are great industries for the spinning of cotton-yarn and the manufacture of cloth, and employ from 10,000 to 12,000 workers. With their many annexes and extensive grounds they cover an area of over one hundred acres on the north-western outskirts of Madras, and by their work are known all over the East.

Wednesday arrived, and once at the mills Mr Turner handed us over to the care of another old friend, Mr Jackson, the able analytical chemist of the mills. Singularly enough, the day of our visit was the anniversary of the day on which twenty-three years before I had married him in the Scots Kirk, Madras. Gratitude as well as friendship made him a splendid guide. Department after department was visited, and we saw the cotton changing by stages from the raw material to the finished article. It was an amazing revelation of what European enterprise and management, combined with Indian workpeople, can do. Most impressive of all the sights was the vast building where 1200 looms were simultaneously at work. It seemed like whole acres of industry. One was stunned and overwhelmed by the mighty activities, the ceaseless whirr, and the great mass of skilled Indians who were carrying it all through. Verily this is an India that is absolutely new, and it has come to stay.

But to us, more significant even than the mills, was the splendid provision made by the Management for the wellbeing and education of the Indian workers. Sir Clement Simpson, the chief representative of the company in India, has made this his special care; and these mills are famous throughout India for this philanthropic side of their activities. For the mill-workers an extensive model village has been built, where the houses are such as the workers never knew before. Splendid school buildings have been erected for the education of the half-timers at the mills, and for the other children of the workers. Four trained and devoted lady teachers from Britain have been brought out, and the equipment of these schools is perfect in every detail. One felt in going round this wonderful place how much superior the equipment was to that with which most *Mission* schools had to be satisfied, and what a field Christian philanthropists have in the Mission schools if they only knew it! No definite religious teaching is given in these schools of the mills, but there are Sunday

Schools, which are largely attended by the young people —and not by Christians only.

Sometimes one hears hard things said as to the 'callousness' of European employers in India concerning the welfare of their employees. There may be cases of this, and there probably are, but I do not hesitate to say they are exceptional. My experience and observation indicates that in concern for the welfare of their Indian employees the Europeans are far ahead of employers who are themselves of Indian blood, and of this the Buckingham Mills is one convincing example.

Yet these same mills, little more than a year before, had been the scene of strikes and riots and bloodshed. Agitators from 'Non-Co-operation' centres had come and told the workers fairy tales of how they had only to cease work and the mills would speedily be their very own, as the present masters would be forced to abandon the whole enterprise. So they ceased—and tried to make those cease who would not. Then came trouble, and for a time racial bitterness that blinded the workers as to their best friends. Happily the trouble passed, and by the time of our visit there was peace and activity on every side.

On the way back we visited an outlying school of our Women's Mission at PULIANTOPE, a little village where some of the mill-people live. During the riots it had suffered badly. The people of the village had soon seen their folly in striking, and wished to return to work, but desperadoes came and burned down their houses. The school had been deserted by many through fear, but now it had largely recovered. It is a school for the poor, and what makes it of peculiar interest is that it is carried on by the contributions of the teachers in the Church of Scotland Mission Schools throughout Madras. They supply the funds, and they are responsible for the management. It is a Mission School for

Indians, and worked entirely by Indians. As such it is a humble forerunner of what will one day be the universal practice in Christian India.

. . . .

It was with increasing regret that we saw those Madras days slipping away, for, as already said, in Madras we were at home ; and our good host and hostess had made that feeling daily stronger. So had our many other friends by their hospitable kindnesses, of which none was more gratifying than a large gathering of missionary friends, old and new, held at the end of our visit in College Park, the suburban home of Mr and Mrs Meston. Some sixty missionaries were there, the combined staffs of the United Free Church Mission, the Christian College, the Women's Christian College, and the Mission of the Church of Scotland. Of the whole number present, there were only some twelve or fourteen who had been in Madras when we had said farewell in 1904. Retrospective talks and speeches were abundant and very pleasant. The aspect of the missionary company had changed considerably. To me it seemed they were all much younger than such a gathering used to look twenty years before. But that, I suppose, only meant that I looked on with older eyes. What really mattered was that there was no lessening of the old earnest purposefulness that marks the true missionary. That was a happy conviction to carry away from Madras when we said 'good-bye,' as very reluctantly we did on Friday, 27th January, when we took train for our next halting-place—Arkonam.

CHAPTER XXIV.

ARKONAM—WHERE THE HEART SPEAKS.

THE heart does not always speak in India to-day. When East greets West there is often a strange constraint that renders the spoken words a very imperfect expression of the heart's real feeling. But at ARKONAM there was no constraint. East met West, and the heart poured out its greeting in words of such joyous welcome and in acts of such brotherly enthusiasm, that the memory thereof will remain a perpetual feast to us two pilgrims so long as life lasts.

On the afternoon of Friday, 27th January, we arrived at the station, and as soon as the train came to a halt the platform opposite our carriage was thronged with a dense crowd of Indians, who greeted us with three ringing cheers. Stepping out, we were met with hearty words of welcome, garlands were hung round our necks, hand-grips of right good will were exchanged with the representative Christians, and with a number of the Indian gentlemen of the town. Outside the station we found that a formidable procession had been arranged; and having taken our place in a motor, kindly lent and driven by Dr Scudder of the American Arcot Mission, a start was made. The route was through the main streets of the town to the Mission Church. A long line of Indian Christians, adults and youths, led the way, carrying banners which bore inscriptions of devotion to the Church of Scotland and welcome to her messengers. Midway in the procession were representative citizens, church-workers, and Mr Silver, and after them the motor and its occupants, which was followed by another steadily-increasing line. Every verandah held its crowd of interested onlookers. A band in front proclaimed the joy of the Christians. At stage after stage there was a halt opposite the house of some Christian, when men or women, boys or girls, came forward with yet another garland, the placing of the garlands being accompanied by spontaneous applause from the spectators, Hindu and Christian alike. Eight times in all did we stop, under arch after arch did we pass, all adorned with striking words of welcome; and at last, each of us bearing a mass of garlands so superimposed as to threaten our powers of speech or even respiration, we reached the church. Here a very short but impressive service was held—the 103rd Psalm, a prayer by the Indian pastor, and the Benediction, pronounced by the Commissioner from Scotland. This last was the culminating act to which all led up; and when it was over, with three hearty cheers we were sped on our way to the Mission House.

I have told this episode at greater length than may seem necessary, but it is told with a purpose. In our whole tour this was the most moving episode of its kind. Very Eastern? Yes; and that is the point of it. The 'welcome-programme' was entirely planned by the Indian Christians. Mr Silver had urged restraint, but they would none of it. "This is our business," they said. "They are our visitors, and we will welcome them in our own way!" And they did so; and their way, India's way, is a good way. As I interpreted that wonderful outburst, it expressed a variety of things, all very pleasing. It spoke of the gladness with which the Arkonam Church welcomed this personal touch with the Mother Church in Scotland; it told of the spirit of friendliness of many Hindus to the Mission and its work; it evidenced the happy relations prevailing, in this part at least of South India, between Indian and European; and indirectly, but convincingly, it witnessed to the very high place in the esteem of the community held by our Church's missionary—for only where this is the case could demonstration so remarkable have been devised and carried out.

Next morning there took place what may be regarded as the 'official' reception. The school was filled with Indian Christians and some Hindu friends. At the far end was erected a platform, on which we two had honoured seats. At one side was a choir and small orchestra (violin, hand-harmonium, and Indian drum), and for twenty minutes we had music, Indian as well as Western. Then came an address well conceived and expressed, read by the head-master of the High School, which told of the present condition of the Mission (805 baptised members, 305 under instruction, and a great number of 'inquirers'; 1 High School, 15 Elementary Schools, and 42 workers). It also told of the hopes of a new High School, which are now being realised, and the need for a hostel for Christian boys, and expressed the gratitude of all to the Church afar for her long and great kindness. The address, beautifully printed on silk, was presented in a small casket of inlaid Indian wood. To reply was a privilege as well as a pleasure. One felt in the midst of friends; and that feeling grew stronger every hour that we remained in Arkonam.

. . . .

Arkonam lies forty-two miles west of Madras. It is an important railway centre, and is surrounded by a wide agricultural district, with a population of over 200,000 people. These are mostly peasants, and include a large number of the humblest agricultural labourers, the village serfs of Hinduism. Here our Mission has for many years carried on work, from Madras as a centre, but only since 1900 has a European missionary been stationed in Arkonam itself. Alas! still only one missionary forms the European staff, though happily he is a host in himself. And the Indian Christian community of Arkonam know it. "He has endeared himself to one and all by his open affectionate heart, and by his untiring zeal and devotion to work; our only fear is he is overworked." So ran a touching tribute they paid in one of the many addresses I received. The work follows the usual recognised lines. There are the schools in the town, the evangelistic and elementary educational work in the district, and the central congregation in Arkonam itself with its numerous activities. In the four glorious days of ceaseless work and continual gladness that we spent at Arkonam we saw something of all the work, a great deal of some parts, and felt all the time that we were among a people where keenness in the work was taken for granted, and where happy brotherliness abounded to an unusual degree.

. . . .

Of *Schools* in the town there are four—the High School, with 272 pupils; an Elementary School connected with it, having 180 pupils; a Girls' School, with 130 on the roll; and a school for the boys of the depressed classes, with 80 pupils. We saw them all. In every case there was good work being done, and in every case too one felt an atmosphere of vigorous pressing on to yet better things. Specially was this the case in the High School, where the enthusiastic young Christian head-master, Mr R. A. Manuel, M.A., L.T., with a staff of eight assistant-masters, is eager for the good name of the school, and this as much in its higher life as in intellectual achievements. In every class-room hung a 'Roll of Honour,' whereon were written the names of the boys who had been first in each subject at the end of the preceding term. There is keen competition for a place on that Roll. All round the walls were mottoes—pithy moral maxims, such as in my own school-days used to head the pages in our 'copy-books,' and which one remembers, and tries to profit by, to this day. So may it be with the Arkonam boys who daily read the mottoes on the class-room walls! That the school is up to date in other things than morality was indicated by the presence of a vocational class for telegraphy—a keenly-appreciated departure in this railway centre.

The fifty-fifth anniversary of the High School fell to be celebrated during our visit. With it was combined the annual prize distribution, and a most memorable meeting was held in the large town hall. Recently an 'Old Boys' Association' had been formed, and they had taken the proceedings in hand. Rs. 150 had been collected, and the whole proceedings were carried through with splendid enthusiasm and with a royal disregard of either time or money. From 4 o'clock to 5 o'clock light refreshments, tea, aerated waters, &c., were served to the company gathering in the compound outside. By 5 P.M. the hall was simply packed with 1000 people—young and old of every race, boys and girls, men and women, Hindu, Mohammedan, and Christian. Indian gentlemen were there in large numbers, so too representatives of the railway community. The programme is an interesting indication of what an Indian community in a country town arranges when it lets itself go. Here are the items: (1) 'O God, our help in ages past!'; (2) Presentation of Address from the 'Old Boys' Association' and the citizens of Arkonam; (3) Recitations by pupils; (4) Drill; (5) Indian fancy costumes (a series of Indian character-sketches); (6) Tamil song; (7) Sleight-of-hand exhibition by a boy; (8) Hindustani song; (9) Trial scene from the 'Merchant of Venice' (admirably done by 'old boys' in rich apparel); (10) Annual report by the head-master; (11) Distribution of prizes (by Mrs Ogilvie); (12) Address by the President (the Church's Commissioner); (13) Votes of thanks; (14) 'God save the King!'

How is this for a programme? It took three full hours to get through, and in all that time hardly one man or boy or woman or girl left the hall. It was an amazing function, Indian to the core, and thoroughly enjoyable by West as well as by East. Best of all was the cordiality and enthusiasm and true friendliness that were universally in evidence. Whatever else the Arkonam High School may do—and it does much else—it is a wonderful agency for goodwill among men.

. . . .

To visit the *District Work* was impossible in the time, so men from the district and women with them came into Arkonam to visit us. One afternoon in the wide verandah of the Mission House, Mr Silver and I sat for several hours as deputation after deputation came from ten of the villages around,—where little communities of Christians now exist, where the evangelist and the missionary are frequent visitors, where humble village schools are doing their useful work, and where by these and other means men and women from the long-despised communities are now being lifted up to a new life and filled with a new hope. It was very touching as group after group came forward, were introduced, sat down, and talked—the men with me, Mr Silver interpreting; the women with my fellow-pilgrim—Miss M'Lean, our old friend from Sholinghur, interpreting. One had seen the class from which they came, and one noted now with gladness what the inbreathing of Christian life had done. They were humble folk still, and always will be, horny-handed sons of honourable toil, and daughters of honest labour; but they are *men* and *women* now, no longer serfs to be trodden underfoot. And Christ has done it!

Ay, and there are hundreds, even thousands, in this area eager to come in. "Our difficulty in the Arkonam field," said Mr Silver in words that burn still, "has been how to keep out many of those who want to come in!" It is an extreme way of putting things, but it is true. Give to the speaker a like-minded colleague, give him a staff of Indian workers who will educate and train these willing recruits, give him the necessary little schools and humble churches, give him a hostel for humble Christian lads of promise, give him, in short, the means that will ensure that such an influx of the lowly and degraded will not result in a lowering and degrading of the life and place of the infant Christian Church—and the Church in Arkonam will increase as did the Church in Jerusalem in the first days.

. . . .

What *the Church* is at its chief centre we saw on the Sunday of our stay, 29th January. It was a great day in the history of the Arkonam congregation. Not only was there this visit from Scotland, but there was also the meetings in Arkonam that week of the Madras Synod of the South India United Church, and there was, most important of all, the ordination of their new minister, the Rev. John Paul Manasseh. Three events, such as are never likely to synchronise again; and the service held in the delightful church that forenoon will long be remembered. Of course the church was packed, and packed it remained for three full hours. We began at 9 A.M., and it was past noon when the services ended. First, we had the usual Sunday service, when a very eloquent sermon was preached by one of the Synod members, the minister of the Royapuram Tamil Church; then the baptism of a whole family—father, mother, and child—by Mr Silver; thereafter the solemn ordination of Mr Manasseh by the Presbytery, and his induction to the pastorate; then an address by myself to the new minister, who struck one most favourably, followed by a vigorous address to the people by the Rev. Mr Peters, the able and sagacious clerk of the Synod; finally, prayers, a hymn, and the Benediction! It was a long but entirely fitting service, and all was conducted in a reverent spirit and an orderly manner. The United Church has not yet thought about uniformity of dress. The Indian ministers of the Arcot Mission (American) wore white gowns, while those of the Scots Missions adhered to the traditional black Geneva robe. To my mind the white robe suited the wearers better than the black, but in the South many of the ministers (from the Congregational wing of the Union) wear no special robe at all.

In the evening of the day the church was filled with quite another congregation—Europeans, Eurasians, English-speaking Indian Christians, and a number of the members, both Indian and American, of the Synod. It was a pleasure to officiate that night, and realise once more how in Christ all nations blend, and find their unity.

. . . .

The last day of this engrossing visit came on Wednesday, 1st February, and still the enthusiastic friendliness of all showed no abating. In the afternoon a farewell 'At Home' was given by the Christians of the Arkonam district, in the open plain adjoining the Mission House, when there was a sumptuous tea, much conversation, amusements for the young folks, and finally an address by Mr Manuel, which deeply touched us two pilgrims by the warm appreciation he expressed on behalf of all for our visit. A walking-stick, with suitable inscription, was presented to me, and a charming small silver bowl to my wife, for which we each gave grateful thanks. Then came many warm hand-grips, accompanied by words of genuine regret at parting, and the last great gathering of this great visit ended. But it was not quite the last. Our train left for Bangalore at 10 P.M., and when we reached the station it was to find that a host of our Indian friends, some Hindus as well as the many

Christians, late although the hour was, had gathered there to say a last 'good-bye'! Hand-shaking all round, a long strong grip of the hand of our pattern host, Mr Silver, the beloved friend of all, and then, with cheers of 'God-speed' ringing in our ears, and making glad music in our hearts, we left Arkonam, where the hearts of men had spoken out so well.

CHAPTER XXV.

ARKONAM—AN INDIAN CHURCH SYNOD.

It was a piece of great good fortune that while we were at Arkonam the Madras Council (or Synod) of the South India United Church happened to be there in session. At Allahabad we had seen the General Assembly of *The Presbyterian Church in India.* Now, through this Synod, one had pleasant intercourse with a yet larger organisation, *The South India United Church,* which embraces all the congregations in South India connected with the Presbyterian Missions—and more also. This Church was formed in 1908 by the linking up of the congregations of the Scottish and American Presbyterian and Congregational Missions in South India. A scheme of Union was adopted which conserves the best elements in both systems. Ordination is by the Presbytery, and the government is by Councils, so the Presbyterian Churches are in a congenial environment. The community it represents numbers over 200,000, and congregations are scattered all over South India, from Travancore to Madras. There are eight Councils or Synods under a General Assembly, and of these eight, this, which met at Arkonam, is one.

There is a strong family resemblance between all Synods, and one found it here as elsewhere. An amiable Moderator occupied the chair, while a keen competent clerk really guided the business. Greetings from the Church of Scotland were given, and most cordially received, and the personal intercourse was very pleasant. But what makes this meeting most worth recording here is the light it threw on the *Indian* attitude towards two important questions which now confront the Church in India. The Synod had thirty-five members. Of these, thirty were Indian ministers or elders, three were American missionaries, two were Scottish (Mr Silver of the Church of Scotland, and Mr Sutherland of the United Free Church, from Chingleput).

One of the important questions concerned the much-urged *Devolution of part of the Missions' operations to the control of the Indian Church.* Already considerable advance had been made towards the framing of an experimental plan. It was practically one that had been tried and proved to be good in the Arcot Mission, and now was proposed for wider application. Under it the Elementary Schools and the Evangelistic Work in the country districts will be guided in future by the Presbytery through a series of graded Committees, on which the Missions are duly represented. The experiment was approved for five years in the first instance, when its continuance would depend on the success which had attended it. All will wish the step complete success, in which case there will be many more steps of the kind to follow. The only difference of opinion that found expression was over the recommendation that during these five years there should be a Committee of Reference, composed chiefly of missionaries, which could, in an extreme case, *veto* any proposal that seemed too hazardous or too costly. Objection to this came not from any of the Indians but from one of the missionaries, who had a rooted dislike to 'safeguards'; but the objection was not pressed, and the scheme was launched.

More difficult and of wider general interest was the other question discussed—that of the *Union of the South India United Church with the Indian section of the Church of England in South India.* Since 1919 Committees of these two Churches have been conferring on this difficult matter, and considerable progress has been made. The scheme advanced and urged by the Anglican side is practically the Lambeth Scheme—mutual 'commissioning' of the ministers of each Church by the other uniting Church; but the commissioning of the Presbyterian ministers to take the form of ordination by bishops—save where these ministers are willing to confine their ministry to their present spheres. A 'Constitutional Episcopacy' seemed to be not unacceptable to the Synod—*i.e.*, an Episcopacy where the bishops should be appointed by and responsible to the General Assembly. But the ordination difficulty, and the uncertainty of the future relations that would obtain with those Churches with which they held at present full communion (*e.g.*, the Scottish Churches), made many of the brethren hesitate.

To me, as a deeply-interested onlooker, it seemed that the majority of the members had not really grappled with the questions at issue, and I felt that a wise decision was come to when a small Committee was appointed to expiscate the points that really matter; and a special meeting of the Synod was summoned for July to consider this, and this alone.

As to the probabilities, it is not easy to pronounce. If this Synod is typical of all the Synods, I should say that there are a few able Indian ministers who are keen for Union, and are willing to go any length in securing it ; there are a few who are keenly opposed to Union, on any basis that will involve the practical denial of the full ecclesiastical status of Presbyterianism ; and there are very, very many who have no keen feelings on the matter, but who would prefer to go on as they are doing. It was significant that from the Travancore Council, which represents one-half of the whole membership of the Church, the answer which came to an inquiry from the General Assembly as to its views ran as follows : "While the Travancore Church Council keeps an open mind with regard to Union with the Anglican and the Mar Thoma Syrian Church, it is at present so engaged with domestic problems that it regrets it has not been able to give full consideration to the question of this wider union."

This is not the spirit that leads to Union. Yet one never knows what may happen in such matters in India. In the history of the only really indigenous Indian Church—the Syrian Church of Malabar—there have been fateful Unions accomplished, when to them the whole Church was apathetic or even antagonistic, and yet was finally led by the strong advocacy of an earnest and determined few. Probably when Lambeth goes further, and recognises frankly the full validity of other ordination than Episcopal, South India will go further too. Then, without sacrifice of any principle, and without any weakening of the ties that link the South India United Church with the Mother Churches of the West, Union will come. That will be a glad day for South India, and for Indian Christianity.

Women of Arkonam Congregation.

Men of Arkonam Congregation.

CHAPTER XXVI.

BANGALORE AND SECUNDERABAD—GATEWAYS OF TWO KINGDOMS.

Two of the leading Native States in India are Mysore and Hyderabad. Elsewhere they would be called Kingdoms. Mysore in area almost equals Scotland; Hyderabad is one and a third times as large as England. Over the one rules a Maharajah, and over the other the Nizam; but they are both really Kings. At what may be termed the gateway of each kingdom is an important city with a large British garrison, and in each city is a Scots Kirk.

I.

BANGALORE is a delectable place in which to live. In the centre of the Mysore plateau, at an elevation of 3000 feet, midway between the eastern and western coasts of Southern India, it enjoys for nine months of the year a charming climate, so congenial to flower as well as to man that the name 'Garden of India' has been given to the station. Regiments love to be posted here, and large numbers of the domiciled Anglo-Indian community retire here. There is thus a permanent civil, as well as a transitory military, population, who require the ministry of the Christian Church. Many denominations are represented by the churches that have been built, and most prominent of all these is the stately St Andrew's Church, which, with its noble tower, challenges the attention of every visitor. Here, in the old days, we two pilgrims had spent nine years of happy service, and it was with lively satisfaction that on Thursday, 2nd February, we found ourselves once more in Bangalore, enjoying the bountiful hospitality of Mr and Mrs M'Neill, the present chaplain and his wife.

Six days were spent in this charming station. Happily they were not overcrowded, and gave time to look around and see the changes, as well as to work off heavy arrears of correspondence. The change most noticeable was one observed in many Indian cities—the passing of many of the old European houses and even localities into the occupancy of Indians. It was one more indication of the advancing Indian and the receding European.

The Kirk has had many vicissitudes since we were here twenty-four years ago. Ebb and flow have succeeded each other more than once. Lately there had been a serious ebb, partly consequent on the departure of a Scottish regiment; but Mr M'Neill was having the satisfaction of seeing a gradual return of the tide. On the Sunday morning we had a goodly attendance at Communion, and in the evening a really fine congregation. Many old friends were there, though not so many as we had found at Madras. But here the interval of absence had been much longer. By the kindness of our hosts we met most of these old friends one afternoon at a Garden Party, and if the years did not roll away as completely as they had done in Madras in like surroundings, it was because in this favoured climate all the generations continue to abide. So we found the little children now grown into mothers, and the mothers we had known transformed into grandmothers. But it was all exceeding pleasant, though sternly convincing that time had not stood still.

Many visits were paid to many things, but three in particular may be mentioned here: they were indicative of much.

One was to *St Andrew's Free School*, where over fifty

of the poorest Eurasian children receive a good elementary education, as well as a daily meal. The erection of the substantial building had been my wife's work many years ago, and it was pleasant to see this bit of the Kirk's philanthropy still going strong. Here, as also in Madras, Calcutta, and Bombay, the care of the poor Eurasian children has long marked the first line of Christian work undertaken by the Scots congregations.

The second sight was not so pleasing. Indeed, it was sadly unpleasing; but it was a sight that the Scots at home should look upon. It was a *closed High School!*

Thirty years ago *St Andrew's High Schools*, a goodly three-quarter square of buildings immediately behind St Andrew's Church, were filled with 240 boys and girls of the domiciled Anglo-Indian community. Admirable work was done in these schools, and from them hundreds of pupils went forth in the course of the years to fill honourable places in the world. The Scots Kirk maintained its inherited reputation as a great educative agency.

Now these schools are closed, and the buildings stand empty! Why is this? Because when times grew hard and expenses multiplied, there was no money to meet the growing costs. Other schools felt the same, but they got help from outside sources. The Anglican school had endowments, and occasional aid from funds at home; the Roman Catholic schools were staffed by nuns and priests whom a 'subsistence allowance' sufficed to maintain. The Scots school had no resources save fees and Government grant. True, the Church at home ultimately gave a little, and the United Free Church generously did likewise. But it was too late, and the help was insufficient, so the schools closed down. It is a melancholy story, but it is a story that has been told in many places in India in recent years, and is in danger of being told in very many more. Anglo-Indian education has never received from the Home Churches the attention and the help that are its due. Only one Church has seen the need, and has poured in its supplies of men and women and schools without stint. That Church is the Church of Rome; and to-day she is reaping her reward in the added membership she is getting from the domiciled community.

Some day—may it be soon!—one hopes and prays that our Scottish Churches will awake to their duty in India to the struggling community of the well-doing people of their own blood and faith. When they do awake these empty class-rooms in Bangalore may once more be filled.

Very different was the third sight we looked upon. It was the *United Theological College*, established in 1910 for the higher training of Indian ministers, and to-day is one of the most famous missionary institutions in South India. It does for South India what Serampore does for the northern half of this vast country; and it works in affiliation with Serampore, its students sitting for the B.D. degree of that old college. *Thoroughness* was written on everything we saw on the day of our visit. Buildings thoroughly adequate, a fine central building for class-rooms and library, study-bedrooms for the students, four excellent houses for the professors, a large beautiful compound for pleasure and recreation—no students of divinity in Scotland study theology under conditions so entirely and thoroughly good as those enjoyed by the divinity students at Bangalore. There were seventeen students in the college on the date we visited, but there is room for thirty-two. Dr Larsen is the principal, but he was away in Denmark, and we had the pleasure of being welcomed by the Rev. Godfrey Philips of the London Mission Society. The Wesleyans and the American Board of Missions supply the other two professors, and truly the students are fortunate in their teachers. And the teachers in their students. A happy hour was spent with them, in 'tea and talk'; and I came away delighted with what I had seen of these young ministers-to-be of the Church in South India. Truly the Indian Church has not stood still, if these men are to be taken as typical of the ministry. They are not, of course, typical *yet*, but they are the advance-guard of what will one day be a great army of ministers, earnest and able, well fitted by training to stand before all India as Defenders of the Faith.

That India needs such men—able in defence and bold in attack—was made very plain on the last afternoon of our stay. Our good host and hostess motored us out away beyond the old city, past the crumbling walls, past the prison cell beside an entrance gate where Sir David Baird was chained to another unfortunate for many weary months by order of Tippu Sultan, and out into the open country to the famous Bull Temple, one of the holy places of Bangalore. There, within a dark and vast temple, a huge boulder had been carved into the shape of a gigantic bull—which on great feast-days thousands come to worship and adore. Verily India needs her Christian theologians.

But one may not live always in a garden, even though it be the 'Garden of India,' and on the evening of 8th February our kind host saw us off on a twenty hours' journey by train to Secunderabad.

II.

SECUNDERABAD is noted for two things—its large military garrison, and its close proximity to Hyderabad city—the capital of the leading Mohammedan state in

India. So far as the Scots chaplaincy is concerned, its visible prosperity depends to some extent on the presence of a Scottish regiment in the station; but even when there is none the small but very loyal 'civil' congregation holds steadily on. Possessing, however, a garrison which is the largest in India after Rawal Pindi, Secunderabad is fairly sure of the recurring presence of the Scottish soldier, and at the time of our visit preparations were busily progressing for the arrival of the 'Royal Scots.' Mr Pitcairn Hill, the chaplain, is a man of great vigour, and with Mrs Hill, whose spirit is equally devoted, and backed by an enthusiastic congregation, he was making things 'hum.' To supply the Church with electric fans and lights a bazaar was held one afternoon during our stay, and with complete success. Another afternoon a special gathering was arranged for the advance party of the Royal Scots, 140 in number, who had just arrived; and in his own breezy way Mr Hill at once captured the soldiers. To me it fell to give three greetings to the company, all of which were warmly received. One was a greeting of gracious remembrance and good wishes, with which at Balmoral, in the previous September, I had been entrusted by the Colonel-in-Chief of the Royal Scots, H.R.H. Princess Mary. It was an honour to deliver it, and to the officers and men it was a joy to hear it. Then came a word of goodwill from the Church at home, also gladly welcomed; and lastly, I took it upon me to greet the lads in the name of the Citizens of Edinburgh. This was tumultuously received, for most of the lads were from Edinburgh, and this was a word from home!

On Sunday we had a fine parade service in the Garrison Church at Trimulgherry, three miles from Secunderabad, where the quarters of the European regiments are; and in the evening in 'St Andrew's' the civil congregation met. It is a charming church, too small for a parade service, but very suitable for the Scots congregation likely to be gathered in Secunderabad. Nowhere was a truer welcome given to the Church's messenger than here. They are a warm-hearted flock, and when the Scottish lads from the regiment begin to find their way here on Sunday evenings they will be made right welcome.

During our stay, in the midst of all the bustle, Mr Hill found time to take us into Hyderabad City, which used to be one of the most intensely 'Indian' of all the cities of the East. It is so in a large degree still, but not as it used to be. Formerly one visited it on the back of a stately elephant; but now the elephants have gone, and the visit is done in a motor-car! More comfortable, but not so picturesque. So too we found it with the changed aspect of one whole section of the city. When last I had seen this part it was a wide extent of squalid close-packed streets and lanes and very humble houses —picturesque may be, but not wholesome. Now all was changed. Some years ago there came a mighty flood, and washed this portion quite away, with the loss of thousands of lives. Now a new view met the eye —a well-built well-planned area, still with many streets and lanes, but such as now furnish models for other Eastern cities. So the once unchanging East moves on. In the higher grades of life it also moves. Formerly the Hyderabad Nawabs had truly fine houses; but now, as one motored along the countryside, the fine houses seemed to have multiplied twentyfold; Indian aristocrats and plutocrats flashed past in their cars every few minutes, and what with the spacious well-kept roads, the beautiful gardens, and the air of prosperity all around, the impression left by Hyderabad was that of a city and a people who are emphatically on the move.

Our base of operations during this visit was a charming one. It was the Hyderabad Residency, which lies half-way between the two cities; and there Colonel and Mrs Knox were our exceedingly kind hosts. Let me tell here a little idyll of Old India, of which the traces still remain in the Residency. On the wall of the drawing-room hangs a painting of two beautiful children of the olden time. They were the son and daughter of a Resident who lived here towards the close of the eighteenth century. One day there fled to the Residency for protection a beautiful young Mohammedan princess, and from the gallant Resident—a Scot, Kirkpatrick by name—she got it, and more also. Resident and Princess fell in love and were married, and 'lived happily ever after.' At least, so long as they lived their happiness was unbroken. But the lady clung to the cloistral life to which she had been accustomed, and behind the Residency her devoted husband got a beautiful garden laid out, with green sward, rich flower-beds, and graceful trees. All round was built a protecting wall, and here his lady loved to come in the cool evenings that succeed the hot days. Here the two children whose picture we saw romped and played beside her, and here the Resident sought a quiet refuge from the many cares of office. To pleasure his wife a little more, and perhaps the children too, a model of the Residency building was constructed some eight feet high, and was placed within the garden, where it still stands. '*The Begum's Garden*' this little retreat of olden time is called. Here one afternoon of our stay, tea was served for our enjoyment, and in this dainty Eden one was carried away back to the old, old India which will never more return. It had its faults, but it had its virtues too; and one of these, beyond all question, was an intimate understanding by East and West of each other's thoughts and ways and needs, compelled indeed by circumstance, but all the same it was an understanding such as now is very hard to reach.

The Begum's Garden, Hyderabad.

Madras Church of Scotland Staff.

Back Row—Mr Mitchell (C.), Miss Evans, Mr Silver (M.), Miss Kelly, Mr Mackenzie (M.)
Front Row—Miss Bain, Mr M'Neill (C.), Mrs Mackenzie, Mrs Ogilvie, Dr Ogilvie, Mrs Mitchell, Miss Forbes.

C. = Chaplain. M. = Missionary.

But once again we had to be up and away, to see a little more of the New India, and the contribution to its welfare which the Christian Church is making. On Monday morning, 13th February, our host and hostess gave us a very kind 'send-off'; at the station Mr and Mrs Hill did likewise; and at a suburban halt we got a third warm good-bye from Mr and Mrs Jamieson, he a son of the manse of Portobello, and a grandson of the famous Dr Bryce of Calcutta. So do Anglo-Indian families hold to India from generation to generation; or must it now be written, 'so *did* they hold'?

CHAPTER XXVII.

POONA—IN THE LAND OF THE MARATHAS.

BUT who are the *Marathas?* They are the people who stand out in India's stormy story as the best fighters whom Hinduism has produced. In the old days of Moghul supremacy the Marathas, under their able but unscrupulous chief, Sivaji, were the only Hindus who bade the 'Great Moghul' successful defiance. Later they were our own tough opponents; and though a century of the *Pax Britannica* has kept their fighting instincts under control, the instincts still abide. So too does the memory of the days when they formed an independent Hindu kingdom, free to harry and to ravage the surrounding States. The name of Sivaji is still a power; and there is little doubt that, should the day ever come when the moderating influence of Britain is withdrawn from India, in the Indian Armageddon that would ensue the Marathas would be in the very thick of the fight. They are a strong people, and able as well as strong. To make them strong for the right, through the influence of the Lord Jesus Christ, is the aim of the Missions that are at work in Poona.

It was three o'clock in the morning when our train reached Poona Station. A most un-Christian hour at which to arrive, but we got an entirely Christian welcome from Mr MacKeggie, our one and only ordained missionary in this field. Mrs MacKeggie repeated it half an hour later when we reached their house; and a few hours' further rest fitted us, when the morning really came, to face the big campaign that had been planned. Though one of the smaller of our 'Men's Missions,' Poona is one of the largest of our 'Women's Missions'; and, as will be seen, the intimate relations obtaining with the Missions of the United Free Church here add to the interest and the importance of the Field. The six days of our stay were utilised to the fullest. Fourteen hours daily was the usual work allowance; so in writing of Poona, more even than of most places, is it necessary to classify the things seen.

I.

The work of our WOMEN'S MISSION is very varied, and it would be difficult to say which part is of the most importance. All parts are good, but none is superior in value to the *St Margaret's Hospital for Women and Children*, where Dr Rose Greenfield and Dr Ara Rankine are in charge, aided by a staff of capable Indian nurses. It was in 1892 that under Dr Lettice Bernard, the devoted founder of the medical work, this hospital was opened; and from the very start it has been oppressed with its own success. Situated as it is right in the middle of the native city, it is easily accessible by patients, and the loving care and far-famed efficiency of which the hospital is the centre make it comparable to the Bethesda Pool, in the number of those who throng to get entrance that they may be healed.

On the morning of our visit, first came a short service with the nurses in the 'quiet room,' where with daily prayer the staff regularly begin their work; thence to the two large central wards, where a brief service was held for the patients. As a rule these wards are 'Purdah,' but I was thought a 'safe' man, so was admitted, and the patients did not object. Here Dr Greenfield interpreted, and the 'congregation' was most orderly. But what a congregation! The wards were crowded and overcrowded, beds were where passages ought to be, and in these passages little convalescents tumbled over each other in their eagerness to see if not to hear. Everywhere were evident the loving care of the doctors and the confidence of the patients. It is verily a Bethesda, and the doctors, with all their skill, do not disdain to let Nature work a cure unaided when she can do so. The bell rang for us to go upstairs to the doctors' quarters for breakfast. "Wait a minute," said Dr Greenfield; "you must see our baby fed!" So we waited. Into the ward was led a goat. A nurse came forward carrying a tiny Indian baby, whom she held up to suck milk from the goat, which was done with much avidity! It was an amazing sight, surely a new idea in baby-feeding. Dr Greenfield explained that great difficulty had been found in rearing 'bottle babies' whose mothers had died. She had heard of this 'goat-mother' plan as being followed in some villages, and tried it here with a very ailing little one, and with complete success. Now the plan is being used by her with many difficult cases, and usually remarkably successfully. There is certainly no possible adulteration of the milk. Nature's method of imbibing is closely followed. The ministering goat falls in with it, licks affectionately the foster-child, and the child waxes fat and kicks with joy. A good arrangement all round!

After breakfast we saw the rest of the hospital—the maternity wing, the nurses' quarters, the operating-room—a new and excellent addition,—the rooms for paying patients, and various accessory buildings. And when at last we came away it was with this main impression: this Poona Hospital is the most *intense* bit of Women's Hospital Work we have yet seen in India; and at the same time, and largely because of this, it is the hospital that most needs extension. Other hospitals no doubt may equal it in the devoted enthusiasm and consecrated skill of the doctors. Many of them do, for happily these priceless qualities are very general in medical missionaries. But so far as we have seen, their buildings and equipment are equal to their needs—or are in process of being made equal, as at Kalimpong. In Poona it is otherwise. The work is glorious, the workers are splendid, and the site is ideal; but the space is not adequate, nor are the buildings. A large scheme of reconstruction, on a scale adequate to the needs which the hospital's very success has made clamant, is what is really called for. It is a rare opportunity for some great-hearted Christian benefactor. Short of that, the Church will do its best little by little to add and improve, but the big thing would be the best thing.

As a Mission agency, the *Orphanage*, as the Poona Boarding School for Christian Girls is termed, has an importance quite equal to that of the hospital. The name is perhaps a little misleading now, though it is a reminder of what the institution was at its beginning in 1865. To-day it houses others besides orphans, and serves the same wide purposes as do the boarding schools in our other Fields. Here Miss Edwards was in charge of the seventy girls whom it contains; and no more needs to be said than that in devoted management, in spacious buildings, in entirely adequate class-rooms and dormitories, and in the manifest happiness of the girls, it is quite abreast of the Calcutta Boarding School at Cossipore.

So too was it with the *Day Schools* in the city, which I saw through the eyes of my fellow-pilgrim. There are in all five such schools, and to two of these was she taken one day by Miss Wallis Smith. In one there were 100 pupils, in the other 115; and in both the work was as thorough as we had seen elsewhere. "And the buildings?" I asked. "As good as in Madras, and better than in Calcutta," was the satisfactory reply. There is still another school for girls in Poona, but its story comes later. Altogether it is a big educational work the Women's Mission does in Poona and the district. At eleven centres some 800 Indian girls are getting a Christian education, in giving which no fewer than forty teachers are employed.

Twenty miles west of Poona lies the upland hamlet of PAUD, where for twenty-two years Miss Harvey has given her strength and means for the uplift of the people. There is a light railway now, by which, if one has ample time, the journey may be made; but we had not, so we went by motor. Mr and Mrs MacKeggie and Miss Wallis Smith accompanied us on what proved a delightful run. Leaving the city we passed first through a limited cultivated area, on the left of which rose a commanding hill, crowned by a great temple. It is the famous temple of Parvati, built by the Peishwa Balaji Baji Rao in 1749 at a cost of Rs. 1,000,000. Within the temple is a silver image of Siva, who supports on one knee a golden image of Parvati, his wife, and on the other a golden image of Ganesh, his elephant-headed son. This is the chief shrine of Hinduism in the whole Poona area. We looked, and hastened on to quite another shrine. Soon the aspect changed, and we were driving through a bare undulating district, which grew increasingly picturesque as we neared the region of the hills. At the entrance to this region lies Paud. It is a small village, with a Government hospital, and other modest official buildings on the level of the road. On a little higher ground is the best sight of all—the chaste little church with its belfry, built by Miss Harvey in memory of her sister. The whole scene reminded one of a Highland moor at home, with few trees, a wide expanse of brown sun-dried grass, the encircling hills, and the *kirk*. Alas! the kirk here is still for the few rather than for the many, for the people are not easy to move. Still they move; and with a little congregation of women (mostly) and the boys and girls of the little school, we had a cheering service that day.

It was Miss Harvey's last week in Paud, though one hopes only for the present. Her life has been one of great devotedness—the solitary European in this remote glen, witnessing and working for Christ through more than a score of years. One knows that the witness and the work will not go unrewarded.

The *Men's Mission* of our Church in Poona is of very recent date, and so far as the presence of an ordained missionary goes, it has been very intermittent. Its first inception was due to the desire of the Women's Mission to see some work for boys and men carried on in this field by their own Church, which would also give them the strength of an ordained colleague's presence. And at present this latter is still an important consideration. But Mr MacKeggie, who has recently gone to Poona with rich experience gained in the Panjab, sees a wide field open before him in which as yet the labourers have been few. Poona has its 'depressed classes' as well as the Panjab, and these have been largely untouched by Missions. In a small humble village just outside Poona we saw a little primary school where some seventy children of this class were being taught. It was a most heartening sight. The master was simply an incarnation of enthusiasm, and the way in which he had managed to inspire these lowly lads and lasses with his own keenness was marvellous. No high-caste school could have done better than the children did that day. One did not marvel that the missionary sees great possibilities once he has mastered the language, and with his Indian catechists and teachers works out towards Paud. And in Poona itself, apart from evangelistic developments, there are things waiting to be done for *Christian* boys ; but for this, co-operation with others is a necessity. In a meeting of our *Mission Council* held one afternoon all these and other possibilities were discussed, and one hopes that the discussion may prove to have been helpful.

II.

Poona has long been the centre of a vigorous and well-staffed Mission of the *United Free Church of Scotland.* At the present time the Mission's most widely-known representative is Dr MacNicol, whose mastery of Indian mysticism is exceptional, and whose practical kindness remains a very pleasant memory of these Poona days. One forenoon, under his guidance, I was enabled to see four of the Mission's leading activities. One was the oldest *Girls' School* of the Scottish Missions. It dated from 1834—the year before the Poona Mission was transferred by the Scottish Missionary Society to the Church of Scotland. Nine years later the school, with all the rest of the Poona Mission work, became the care of the Free Church of Scotland ; and now, at the advanced age of seventy-eight years, I found it still 'going strong.'

The same verdict may be given on a much younger institution visited—the *Training Institute for Teachers.* To this all missionary Poona is indebted, for it is here that the senior girls pass from most of the Mission schools who wish to be trained as teachers. Several girls from our own schools were here in training, and everything bore the impress of thorough efficiency. Miss Gordon is the lady in charge, but unfortunately for me she was absent in Calcutta at a conference at the time of my visit, so I did not see one whose praise is in all the Missions.

The *Hospital,* which we also visited, is a first-class building, a large two-storey central block, with extensive wings and numerous other adjuncts. Of all the hospitals we had seen, the U.F.C. Women's Hospital at Madras and this for men in Poona take priority in regard to their structural completeness. But—alas that there should be a 'but,'—the site of this fine building is proving malarial, and both medical staff and patients wish earnestly that the mosquito or other cause could be removed. Then would this hospital be as near perfection as a Mission hospital to-day can be.

Most interesting of all to me, because it was something I had not yet seen in this tour, was the fourth institution visited. This was the *Mission's Aid Printing Press,* a flourishing establishment, where all varieties of printing were done by a large staff of Indian printers, under the management of a capable young Scot from Auchterarder. It is an industrial effort, carried on by a lay company, who hand over all profits above 5 per cent or thereby to the Mission. In the previous year, I believe, the amount thus received by the Mission was Rs. 30,000. Good business! This is not a case of an industry carried on by a Mission. To such a practice there are many who take exception, and not without cause. It often leads to complications with outside industries, and to a secularising of a Mission's life. But this is the case of an independent company, whose promoters are in warm sympathy with Missions, giving thought and energy to the upbuilding of a business on business lines, contenting themselves with a small fixed profit, and handing over the excess for the good of the missionary cause. Would that such companies were multiplied tenfold!

III.

The distinctive feature of these two Scottish Missions in Poona is the extent to which they are worked as one. They are not one—yet; but they are one in spirit, in aim, and in brotherly life—one in their ecclesiastical colour and in the country of their origin, and one in the hope that organic unity will speedily be given by a linking up of the Scottish parent Churches. Meantime, with the cordial consent of both these Churches, there has been formed a *United Advisory Council* of the two Missions, by which the two programmes of work are kept in harmonious accord. Of this very close approach to Union several pleasing evidences and activities came before us.

St Andrew's Girls' (Middle) School was one of these. Here Miss Greenshields takes command, and, needless to say, the school is a success. From the United Free Church Mission come twenty-eight Christian girls, from the Church of Scotland twenty-two, and from other quarters twenty. In all, about seventy girls are taught here, and the controlling Missions, to all intents and purposes, are one. The school meets at present in one half of a large United Free Church building, but negotiations are going on with other missionary societies as to the possibility of establishing a good High School for girls, to be the co-operative work of all the Missions. This will probably soon develop.

Most visible of all the evidences of the Union spirit is the church itself, in which the Christians of both Missions meet for worship. A little while ago each Mission had its own church and congregation; now they have united, and *Nana's Peth Church* is the central sanctuary. It is a spacious building, holding well over 400 people, and on the Sunday afternoon of our visit it was crowded. The girls from both Boarding Schools were there, all the missionaries and teachers, and a host of the regular members of the congregation. Mr Deshpande, the minister, a devoted and able man, took the service, and then interpreted for me when I preached. The church is entirely self-supporting, and contributes a substantial sum to the evangelistic Christian work of Poona. Ecclesiastically it is a congregation of the local Presbytery of the Presbyterian Church in India.

The *Kirk-session* was an interesting body of men, and Dr MacNicol kindly invited us to meet them one afternoon in his house. Several of them spoke their welcome to the visitors; Mr Deshpande made frank acknowledgment of the debt the Indian Church owed to the Churches of the West; and Mr Savarkar paid interesting and warmly appreciative tributes to friends of long ago, the Misses Bernard and Dr Wann. A very fine type of elder is Mr Savarkar, an Indian gentleman who has served long in the upper grades of the Educational Service, drawing a salary of about £1000 a year, and now has retired, and comes to offer valuable honorary service to the Christian Church.

The *Advisory Council* itself held a meeting during our stay, at which one learned a good deal about men and things. Eighteen members were present, the mission-

Group of Patients at St Margaret's Hospital, Poona.

Paud Church, Poona.

aries of both Churches, and two Indian members, Mr Savarkar and Mr Bhaskare, a keen and capable young Indian missionary of the United Free Church. Of most importance was an exposition by Dr MacNicol of the position that had been adopted by the United Free Church Mission with regard to the *Devolution* of part of the Mission's work to the care of the Indian Presbytery. It was the same question which had been discussed by the Synod at Arkonam, and the decision as to the work to be transferred was the same also. All the elementary schools and the district evangelistic work had already been handed over to the care of the Presbytery's Committee; and, said Dr MacNicol, 'I am now a worker under the Indian Presbytery.' One difference there was from the South Indian arrangement. There was no 'Committee of Reference' here with a power of *veto*. The transfer of responsibility and the control of the funds by the Presbytery was here absolute. Of these, one-twentieth comes from the Indian Church, and nineteen-twentieths from the Mission. One felt the greatness of the trust the Mission was showing, and also the greatness of the call to the Indian Church to justify the trust. Dr MacNicol was certain that it would; and no man knows the Indian Church better than he.

So far as the Church of Scotland Mission was concerned, the question hardly arose. Women's work is wholly outwith the Presbytery's care, and our men's work requires time to develop under Mr MacKeggie before devolution can be talked of.

Many other things were discussed that afternoon, all of value; but best of all was the clear evidence the meeting gave of the strong unity of heart and purpose which animated every member.

In Poona, as in most large Indian cities where many

Missions are at work, there is held a monthly *Conference of all the Missionaries*—a happy social gathering at one of the Mission Houses, where after tea and talk some missionary subject is introduced by speech or paper, and afterwards discussed. The Poona Missionary Conference met when we were there, as the guests of Mr and Mrs MacKeggie, at our own Orphanage. Over seventy missionaries and friends were present, whom to meet was a very real pleasure. To me it fell, by previous arrangement, to speak on one's impressions on revisiting India, and the 'discussion' thereafter was generously kind. Many changes there had certainly been in the intervening years, but here, as on a like occasion in Madras, one rejoiced to feel that in missionary devotion there had been no change, and that missionary assurance of ultimate victory was as strong as ever.

CHAPTER XXVIII.

POONA—AND THE PIPES!

POONA holds other Scottish interests than the Scottish Missions. It holds a Scots kirk, a Scots chaplain, a Scots congregation, and, at the time of our visit, it also held a Scots regiment, the 1st Argyll and Sutherland Highlanders. With all these evidences of the Scot being abroad we had right pleasant contacts.

The kirk was the centre—a quite worthy building, not very ornate, but pleasantly situated in the midst of a small encircling grove of trees, and the interior adequate and conducive to worship. Three services we had there: one a helpful and significant Communion

Service on a week-day afternoon, attended by the missionaries of the two Scottish Missions; another on the evening of Sunday, when a goodly congregation, mostly of the civil community, was present; and, best remembered of all, the Parade Service of the Argylls on Sunday morning. That was a great service. Every officer was there, and every Scottish Presbyterian man who was not on duty—for a memorial tablet in honour of the men who died at Poona during the Great War was to be unveiled and dedicated. For the most part, the dead were men who had come back sick or wounded from Mesopotamia, and here had passed away. Now their fellow-soldiers were met to honour their memory in this House of God. Mr M'Caul, the chaplain, shared the regular service with me, and then followed the dedicatory service. All stood while the words of dedication were pronounced, succeeded by the moving 'Last Post' from the bugles and Chopin's funeral march by the band. The music ceased, and still we stood, for from far away came a low wailing note that strangely thrilled every Scottish heart. It was the note of the Pipes, and they played 'The Flowers o' the Forest are a' wede away.' Nearer came the notes of that wonderful lament, and clearer they grew as the music rose and fell. Into the church came ten stalwart pipers, and with measured step, slow and stately, itself a reverent tribute, up the aisle they moved, past the spot where the memorial was now unveiled, and all the time the low sad music was gripping the heart and making moist the eyes of the congregation, who stood thrilled to the very core. Then out into the open went the pipers, and still we stood, until the last notes faded away in the distance. Truly these Scottish dead got a fitting requiem that day in Poona Church. After it was all over Colonel Hyslop, a leal Scottish gentleman, as well as a brave soldier, came to express the thanks of the regiment to the Church of Scotland for the message of affectionate regard which had been given. "Believe me," he said, "we all value it very highly."

Earlier in the week one had met the regiment in another way—at dinner at the Officers' Mess. A more courteous or a more kindly band of officers, from Colonel to the youngest subaltern, the British Army cannot hold. Among them one was glad to meet young Clement Hetherwick, a son of our own Dr Hetherwick of Blantyre. Here again we had the pipers, and they gave us music that touched one quite differently, but quite as strongly. "Is there any tune you would specially like?" asked the Colonel, after we had had a perfect feast of pipe music. "Yes," I replied—"'Monymusk,' the tune that immortalises my own beautiful birthplace." So we had 'Monymusk' played to perfection; and then the Colonel, who himself hails from Donside, gave another order, and as one heard 'O gin I were whaur Gadie rins, at the back o' Benachie,' the hills of home rose up in vision, clear and beautiful as of old, and more alluring than ever.

With the congregation of the kirk we had also a very pleasant social contact, at an 'At Home' very kindly given by Mr and Mrs M'Caul one afternoon. Some seventy guests were there, including a number of the Scottish sergeants and their wives. Among those present was one old European resident of ninety-two years of age. Thirty years previously he had belonged to my congregation in Bangalore, and here he was, hale, hearty, and joyous as ever. "Well, young man," I said, after we had had a long talk, "good-bye, and God bless you." "Good-bye, my boy," was his reply, "and God be with you!" It was very cheering to be so addressed. To ninety-two one is still a 'boy' at sixty.

One whole day while at Poona was given to a duty

Church of Scotland Staff, Poona.

Back Row—Mr M'Lellan (C.), Mrs M'Caul, Mr M'Caul (C.)
Middle Row—Mr MacKeggie (M.), Miss Harvey, Dr Greenfield, Miss Edwards, Dr Rankine, Miss Greenshields.
Front Row—Mrs MacKeggie, Mrs Ogilvie, Dr Ogilvie, Mr Nelson (C.), Miss Wallis Smith.

C.=Chaplain. M.=Missionary.

Parade of 1st Argyll and Sutherland Highlanders at St Andrew's Church, Poona.

that had just as much to do with Poona, and no more, as it had with every other station in India where Scots chaplaincy work is done. This was to attend and take part in the annual *Conference of the Presidency Senior Chaplains* of the Church of Scotland. Over the chaplains in each of the three Presidencies is the Presidency Senior Chaplain, and once every year the three meet to take counsel with each other concerning the general interests and desirable developments of the work in India. This year the place of meeting was Poona, and the time chosen was that of my visit. So we had Mr Drummond Gordon from Bengal, Mr M'Neill from Madras, and Mr Nelson from Bombay. Important questions connected with the chaplaincy work, and with the service in general, were discussed, for these are days of change and development in every Indian service. Resolutions were arrived at of unusual moment, which I was deputed to lay before the Government authorities at Delhi, and later before the Church at the General Assembly in Edinburgh. Of these I do not write here, but the Conference was one of much moment.

So the busy Poona days passed, reaching their end on the Sunday evening. Next morning, 20th February, at 7 o'clock, the ladies of the Mission and our very good host, Mr MacKeggie, were all at the station to wish us 'good-bye,' and with Mr Gordon as travelling companion we were off to Bombay on the last lap of our journey. Yet for me not quite the last. At Bombay I left my fellow-pilgrim in the kind hands of Mr and Mrs Nelson, and that night started with Mr Gordon on a thirty-six hours' journey to Delhi to see the great ones there. They were all exceeding courteous. To meet the Viceroy at luncheon, to have a private interview with the Commander-in-Chief, and to talk over with their leading advisers the points connected with our chaplaincies that needed consideration—were pleasant and useful experiences. Two days and the night between was, however, my Delhi limit, so there was not much time in which to see Delhi itself. But some things I did see. With Mr Gordon I spent one afternoon in the great plain where 'New Delhi' is to arise. Part has already arisen. The general lines of the roads and drives are now laid out, and with the furthering aid of Mr Barron, the Commissioner (another Aberdonian), we fixed on the site where by-and-by a Scots kirk should be built. But the whole project of the new Imperial city is on so vast a scale that one wonders when it will all come to fulfilment. Another Delhi sight, made possible by a rapid motor run, gave touch with the mighty past. It was the famous *Tomb of Humayun*, the father of the great Akbar, ancestor of the mightiest line of Eastern kings whom India has ever known. The stately well-preserved mausoleum befits the stately dead who here are buried, for five of Humayun's successors lie here beside the founder of their line. New Delhi and Old Delhi—how great the contrast! Yet somehow one feels that though the New has indeed come, the Old, in the deepest thought and life and sympathies of the people, has not passed away. With India it is the same. There is a New India, but Old India is with us still.

Back to his delightful and most hospitable bungalow Mr Macpherson—worthy son of Elgin manse—drove us; and that night Mr Gordon and I went our separate ways, he to Calcutta and I to Bombay, leaving the 'City of Kings' behind us for ever.

CHAPTER XXIX.

BOMBAY—HAIL AND FAREWELL!

THE closing week of our Pilgrimage had come, and it was fitting that it should be spent in Bombay. Here five months ago we had halted for a brief hour, and had said to India, *Hail!* Now, in a few more days, we should be looking back from the steamer's deck, and crying from the heart to this wonderful land a regretful *Farewell!* A mighty city is Bombay, and in wealth is equalled by few. In Kipling's 'Song of the Cities' of the Empire he gives Bombay first place and speech :—

> "Royal and Dower-royal, I the Queen
> Fronting thy richest sea with richer hands—
> A thousand mills roar through me, where I glean
> All races from all lands."

Of that last week two impressions dominate. One is the splendid brotherliness of the two Scottish Churches, and the other the boundless hospitality of the Bombay Scots. Among the races which Kipling says the great city gleans, the Scots are prominent, and the sole work of the Church of Scotland in Bombay is with them. For long we had also a Mission College, but its life was never strong after 1843, and over thirty years ago it died.

I.

On Saturday forenoon, 25th February, I had returned from Delhi, and the great service arranged for the following evening in St Andrew's Church struck the note for the whole week, and gave the key to a true understanding of the work for the Scoto-Indian as it is carried on in Bombay. It is a work where Scottish Church divisions are simply pushed into a corner, and the two kirks are as one. On Sunday evening this was visualised in a way that will long be remembered. The United Free Church, by the unanimous decision of the Session, closed its doors. Minister, Session, and Congregation all journeyed to St Andrew's Kirk, and there together we worshipped God as one Scottish family. Everything had been well planned by Mr Nelson—most careful and reliable of chaplains—and by Mr Gray, the much-esteemed minister of the sister Church. Eight ministers were present in their robes, three of our own Church, Mr Nelson, Mr Lee, and myself; and five from the United Free Church, Mr Gray, and four missionaries. Mr Gray, Mr Lee, and Mr Nelson conducted the service, and to me the happy duty fell of preaching and of giving to this splendid Scottish congregation the warm greetings from home. The church was packed, the singing was glorious, and when at the close we sang together, 'Pray that Jerusalem may have peace and felicity,' one felt that a Pisgah view had been granted to us all, of what will be seen in Bombay every Sunday not many years hence. The congregations are *ripe* for union. When the elders met in the Session House before service it was as one body, and at the close it was the same. The welcome given to the messenger from home was of like heartiness from all. From that opening day of our Bombay week I felt that I was already a minister of the larger Church of Scotland that is coming; and when from the United Free Church missionaries came a warm invitation to visit their work, it was as warmly accepted as a thing that simply ought to be.

II.

It is a big Mission which the United Free Church has in Bombay; and the *Wilson College*, which I saw first of all the Mission developments, is a big enterprise. Not so big as the Calcutta and Madras Colleges, but these are 'company' undertakings, while here the United Free Church is sole partner. This is the scene of Dr Mackichan's long and honourable career. Some of his students are still here, and when Mr Mackenzie, his successor in the principalship, took me round the classes, I found that to say I was a friend of Dr Mackichan at once released the willing smiles. But he is happy in his successor—who is able and wise; as any man who comes from Gordon's College, Aberdeen, is expected to be. So at least I may be pardoned for believing—whose father was the 'Maker of Gordon's.' Eight missionary professors form the European staff, and there are many Indian assistants and lecturers. In the college are 550 students, and one was impressed with the strong virile look of these Maratha youths. Man for man, they would be much more than a match for the students of Bengal or Madras in any physical contest; and for general grit I should be inclined to back them too.

The *Wilson High School*, which I saw another day, with its 500 boys, was also a busy place; but one found here, as in not a few other cities, that the changing temper of Young India, as well as the increasing cost of education, is forcing into prominence schemes of co-operation between Missions, whereby in *Schools* the Christian element, both in staff and pupils, may be strengthened, without incurring a financial loss beyond the power of the co-operating Missions to meet. In Bombay especially it was not surprising to hear such things discussed, seeing that the year before there had been a temporary revolt against the Christian teaching in Mission Schools. It was soon ended, but the bad taste remains, and one consequence may well be a development of school co-operation by several Missions.

The High School and Boarding School for Girls, situated

in the centre of what is a fine extensive Mission settlement, was a treat to visit. Eighty girls are educated here—forty Christians and forty Hindus,—an experiment which Miss Sutherland, the able principal, says works well. I was fortunate enough to see a display of Swedish-club exercises by ten of the senior pupils, girls of fifteen or sixteen years of age; and for grace, precision, and suppleness of movement these Maratha maidens eclipsed anything I had seen their sisters do in other parts of India. Again one felt, as in going round the Wilson College, that the Marathas have something in them that many Hindu peoples lack. These young women had character and self-reliance stamped upon their faces, and yet no trace of unmaidenly forwardness. Later in the day we met a number of the leading Indian Christians at an 'At Home' in the Wilson College, and had many interesting talks. Once again one 'sensed' the stamina of the Maratha race. It may well be that with this inheritance of backbone, the Maratha Church of Western India will give a lead in many things to India's other Churches, in provinces where men are, if perhaps more amiable, yet not so strong and virile.

III.

For half a century and more the two Scots congregations have combined to foster the education of the Scottish portion of the domiciled European community; and to-day three schools for this purpose are at work in Bombay—the Bombay Scottish Orphanage, and two Day-Schools under the Bombay Scottish Education Society.

The *Scottish Orphanage* we saw on the Sunday morning. "You are down for the Orphanage in the morning," had been Mr Nelson's warning on Saturday night; and by 8.15 A.M. we were off with him in his motor to Mahim,

Madras.

Bombay.

Calcutta.

Rawal Pindi.

Colombo.

Five Scottish Churches in the East.

nine miles along the coast, where the Orphanage fronts the sea. Once clear of the great city the road gets rather like the palm-fringed roads of Colombo, and the Orphanage looks out on a charming sea-scape. It is a good building, and the fifty boys and girls who are here are very well cared for. Mr Ripley, who worked for a while at Kalimpong, knows his business, and the children have a real *home*. Every Sunday morning they have a service for themselves in the hall, conducted alternately by the chaplain of St Andrew's and the United Free Church minister. That morning I took the chaplain's duty, and very pleasant it was. Even more so was a talk with the boys and girls afterwards. They are a good set of young people, socially much higher than the Kalimpong children, and they do well when school-days are ended and they go out to face the world. The Orphanage was a favourite child of the still-remembered chaplain, Dr Duncan Macpherson, whose portrait hangs upon the wall; and to this day it is a pet child of both the Scottish congregations.

The Day-Schools offer a more difficult problem. They are the care of the *Scottish Education Society*, on whose Committee of Management the two Churches are equally represented, and in the past have done fine work. Both are good schools still. The John Connor School, with 150 boys and girls, under the management of Mr Wilkinson, a born teacher and an enthusiast for education, was a delight to visit, and so too with the Byculla School, under Mr Ross, with its smaller attendance of eighty pupils. But the times are hard, and the pressure from increased costs, aided competition outside, and the ubiquitous Roman Catholic schools,—forces which killed the Scots School in Bangalore,—are telling adversely in Bombay also. Strong and steady aid from the Scottish Churches at home, such as is given for the great missionary colleges, would long ago have saved the situation, but that has never come. Anglican schools are also feeling the pressure; and all are not a little anxious as to the attitude to European education of the new Indian authorities. So now a combination of Anglican and Scottish schools was being talked of, and had almost reached a conclusion when we were there. One grieved to think that the old Scots schools should lose their identity in a new 'combine'; but it seems the only course at the present moment. The whole question, however, calls loudly for the attention of the Churches at home, and the Scots in India ask with pathetic urgency that the attention should be given without delay. These children of our own blood, of parentage as honourable as any child's at home, and of people deserving and respectable, cannot be left alone until they become objects of charity. They must be helped now to continue to hold the honourable place which by inheritance and right is theirs in British India.

The day before we sailed there was held the annual Prize Distribution of these two day-schools, and one had only to look at the children and their parents and friends to feel how very, very strong is their claim upon us. They are bone of our bone and flesh of our flesh.

IV.

Of the strength of the note of Christian unity in Bombay we had many evidences besides those already mentioned. Two meetings in particular must be recorded, one private and the other public, one bearing on Scottish Church union, the other witnessing to the unity of feeling pervading a much wider circle.

The *private meeting* was one that is surely rarely paralleled in Scotland, though it should have many parallels there at no distant date. On the evening of 1st March the Kirk-sessions of both the Scottish Churches met in the vestry of St Andrew's to discuss—what? *How these two congregations can become one, without waiting for the larger union of the parent Churches in Scotland.* But for the links that connect them with home ecclesiastical organisations, and the constitutional difficulties that in consequence exist, these two congregations of true Scottish folk would be one to-morrow. That this would be a great gain for Scottish Christianity in Bombay is manifest to everybody. Neither Church is adequate by itself, but united, and with a new building in a suitable site in its architecture worthy of the Scottish Kirk, Scottish Presbyterianism would be a force in Bombay greater than it has been for many a day. So keen is the desire for union that sites for the new church were being discussed, and other practical matters considered. It was good to talk things over together. The constitutional difficulties in the way of rapid action are just about as great as those which would face a similar proposal in any Scottish parish at the present hour. In India one of the greatest of the difficulties may, however, be soon removed, should changes take place that some expect in the relations of the chaplaincies to Government. But whether thus or otherwise, the Scots in Bombay want union; and I was deputed to bring their desire before the parent Churches in the Motherland—which it will be an uncommon pleasure to do.

The more *public meeting* was of a different kind, and was meant to serve a different purpose. To say 'Hail' and 'Farewell' to the Commissioner of the Church of Scotland and his wife, the St Andrew's congregation had arranged a great Reception in one of the large halls of the city. The ladies of the church, with Mrs Nelson at their head, had taken the matter in hand, and with magnificent results. The hall was beautiful with decorations. Sailors from Commander Lang's ship, which was then in port, sent their willing help in making the walls gay with bunting, and the creature comforts of tea and 'adjuncts' were all that the most fastidious could desire.

Over 200 guests were present, including representatives of all the Churches, and of many sides of European life. The Bishop of Bombay and his wife were there; the Archdeacon; the Chief-Justice, Sir George Macleod, and Lady Macleod; the ministers of the Wesleyan, the Baptist, and other Churches; and, of course, our brethren from the United Free Church and Mission. It was easily the most *representative* gathering of the European community we had met in India, and gave the best evidence on a large scale that we had yet seen, of the true friendliness that pervades the Churches. First came tea, then a brief concert, and thereafter the inevitable but necessary, and here very fitting, speeches. Mr Nelson, in the name of the kirk and the many friends of the kirk, spoke a warm welcome to the two Scottish pilgrims, whose Indian tour was finishing, and to his over-generous words I had to reply. To express thanks was easy. It was both a pleasure and a privilege. But more was needed on an occasion like this. At the Poona Missionary Conference, with its seventy missionaries, one had in effect said farewell to the general missionary body. To-day was practically a 'Farewell' to our British countrymen in India; and I gladly embraced the opportunity to express the warmest appreciation of their high courage and calm steadfastness in very difficult times. All through the tour this had been increasingly impressed upon me. Compared with the Europeans in India in my own old Indian days, those who are there to-day have a difficult life to live. So far as the material comforts of life are concerned they are more richly supplied than we were. It is now the day of the motor-car, thee lectric light, and the electric fan—very superior

Church of Scotland Staff, Bombay.

Mrs Ogilvie, Mr Nelson, Dr Ogilvie, Mr Lee, Mrs Nelson.

Wilson College, Bombay. (U.F.C.)

to the days of 'one-horse shay,' the punkah coolie, and the kerosene oil-lamps. But they have not now the kindly environment that we had, and life is much less 'spacious.' Yet, just as the result of this, there is a note of earnestness in living the life, more widely spread than it used to be. India is challenging the European to be his best and do his best; and the challenge is being met. Nowhere is this truer than with those in whose hands lie the higher responsibilities. The day of the 'little tin gods,' who sported in Simla, Ootacamund, Darjeeling and elsewhere, while workers sweated unconsidered in the plains, is quite gone. Indeed, it never existed save where some individuals were concerned. But now it is a thing inconceivable. The 'gods' who are still there are not gods but men: they are not 'tin' but 'steel,' and sometimes 'gold'; they are not 'little,' but for the most part 'big,' alike in their conception of their duty and their endeavour to perform it. Sometimes the restraining hand of home has made them do things, or leave things undone, at which the world has wondered; but of the men themselves, take them all in all, it is simple justice to say that the type is that which Britain expects to find in her Indian sons—men wise and strong, open-eyed to the changes which a changing India requires, and very willing to make the necessary adaptations, but mindful always of India's vastness and of the right of every section of her people to the protection and the fostering care of the Power that is supreme.

Even so has one found it to be with the great majority of the European community. Some there are no doubt who fall below the common standard as to how the European should 'play the game'; but by most it is well and fairly played. There is a frank acknowledgment of the Indian's right to occupy an ever greater place in the developing of India, and a real desire to clasp his hand in friendship; but there is also a consciousness of the European's own right to a continued place in that Eastern land where Providence has ordered that East and West shall live together, for each other's and the world's good.

Some of these thoughts I tried to express that afternoon in Bombay, and they found ready approval among that fine audience of our fellow-countrymen. Well may Britain be proud of her sons and daughters in India to-day. They are facing the new situation as she would wish them to do—with head held high, with eye clear and fearless, with heart in wise sympathy with India's needs, and with will resolute to 'trust in God and do the right.'

So the Bombay week drew towards a close. Of the hospitalities received every day and every evening I dare not begin to speak. They began at the home of our good friends Mr and Mrs Nelson, and they extended in every direction—through the homes of United Free Church missionaries, Scottish merchants, and Government officials. Had it been possible to kill us with kindness, we had never left Bombay alive. Bombay the Bountiful it will ever be to us.

But Saturday, 4th March, the date for our steamer's departure, came, and the 'good-byes' had to be said. Down to the Ballard Pier we went, accompanied by Mr and Mrs Nelson, Mr Lee, and Mr Mackenzie (the chaplain from Agra, then on his way to Madras). With many regrets at parting, but with happy anticipations of meeting in Scotland, the last farewells were said, and we passed up the ladder-way on to the deck of the good ship *Malwa* that was to bear us home. There one more 'good-bye' awaited us, for Commander Lang, brave sailor son of Stirling manse, had got on board as no common landsman could, and with his as India's last farewell we sailed away. Heartening messages were waiting us on board, from missionaries and chaplains from the Panjab, Calcutta, and Bangalore, all saying kind things and wishing us a prosperous voyage. As the distance from the shore grew steadily greater, we realised that the Indian Pilgrimage had indeed ended, and amid the many thoughts and emotions that surged within us one was dominant—profound gratitude to God for having given us strength every day, and all the days, right through to the very end.

CHAPTER XXX.

THE INDIAN 'ATMOSPHERE.'

LOOKING back on those days of Pilgrimage now ended, I ask myself, What struck you most of all while in India? The answer comes at once. It was the changed 'atmosphere.' From the first day at Karachi to the last day at Bombay, one was conscious of an environment quite unlike that of the India of twenty years before. The atmosphere—mental, spiritual, social, political—in which one moved had elements altogether new and strange. Yet to describe it is not easy, for it varied greatly in different localities and in different communities. The Panjab atmosphere was not that of Madras; the Calcutta atmosphere was not that of the Eastern Himalayas; the atmosphere of the High School and Colleges greatly differed from that of the rural districts; that where the Chuhra lived had almost nothing in common with the atmosphere which enveloped the Maratha. Still amid all the differences there were two elements that, in varying degree, were present almost everywhere; and when one speaks of the Indian atmosphere of to-day, it is these elements that are most present to the mind. They are elements that are making the work of Christian Missions in India exceptionally difficult, but at the same time are giving to that work an extraordinary importance. They are Racialism and Nationalism. A brief chapter indicating what these mean for Indian Missions may fitly close this record of an Indian Pilgrimage.

I.

RACIALISM has India in its grip to-day. This is only to say that India is sharing in the outburst of racial feeling that since the Great War has swept over the whole East like a flood. It had begun before the war, and would have developed had there been no war. But its development has been hastened and its force immensely intensified by the earth-shaking experiences through which the world has passed. The presence of a Western to-day in India is, in the eyes of many, an offence. The innate superiority of the East is with many an axiom. By those who so believe, the logical consequence is held to be the elimination of the West from India, so that the East may have opportunity to live its own life along its own intrinsically superior lines. This is the creed of Mr Gandhi, who sought to carry it into practice by starving the Westerns into a voluntary evacuation of India, through the process termed 'Non-violent Non-Co-operation.' His followers have showed that this method does not work out just as their idealist leader expected. Human nature being what it is, the 'non-violence' ingredient in the prescription soon dropped out. Violence of an ugly kind was freely and disastrously substituted, and has had to be suppressed. But the spirit of Racialism, the antagonism of East to West, of which Gandhi-ism was only one outcome, still abides; and seeing that the British are to India the representatives of the West, on them falls the brunt of the racial outbreaks both in word and deed. Any other Western people occupying our place in India to-day would be similarly treated. It is not because we are *British* that our presence in India is objected to by the extremists: it is because we are *Westerns.*

What this means for Missions, carried on by missionaries from the West, can readily be imagined. The people among whom much of their work is done, the people of the villages and the lower classes in the towns, are those most easily influenced by the political agitator or the racial fanatic. They have not the knowledge and the wide outlook that make the crude methods of Non-Co-operation impossible to Indians of light and leading, and to Indians of the best type more than impossible, even abhorrent. By whispered word, by printed tract, by a cheap and widely-circulating vernacular Press, the anti-Western spirit is fostered; and again and again the missionaries feel its hostile influence. "We are getting now in the Panjab," said to me a missionary of long experience, "a little taste of what our missionaries in China have had all along."

This is not *Nationalism. It is Racialism.* Nationalism at its best is a mighty force for good; Racialism is never anything but a power for evil. There is Nationalism at work in India too, powerfully at work in the hearts and minds of some of the very best of India's sons. But not, as I read the situation, in India as a whole. India's *national* life is only beginning, and how fast and how far it will proceed depends on many things. Most of all does it depend on a frank recognition by all who wish that India may finally become a nation, of the long way that has to be travelled, and of the many difficulties that have to be overcome. On this vexed but vital question it is better, however, to let sons of India speak, and with quoting the weighty words of two I content myself.

Here are words of an Indian sage, addressed last year to the Universities of North India, through a most thoughtful anonymous book, *India's Destiny*, which throbs with love of country :—

> "India, lacking discipline, lacking a national soul, with her hundred divisions and antipathies, with her immaturity of mind and purblind enthusiasm, is fast moving to one goal, and one goal only—chaos. . . . There are only two ways of India attaining nationhood: one is through self-discipline, the other through a blood-bath. The greater consciousness can only be born through either of these two ways—discipline, or the wisdom that comes through suffering."

To this let these words of Rabindranath Tagore be added :—

> "When our Nationalists talk about ideals, they forget that the basis of Nationalism is wanting. The very people who are upholding these ideals are themselves the most conservative in their social practice. Nationalists say, for example: Look at Switzerland, where, in spite of race differences, the people have solidified into a nation. Yet remember that in Switzerland the races can mingle, they can intermarry, because they are of the same blood. In India there is no common birthright, and when we talk of Western nationality, we forget that nations there do not have that physical repulsion for the others that we have between different castes. Have we an instance in the whole world where a people who are not allowed to mingle their blood, shed their blood for one another—except by coercion, or for mercenary purposes? And can we ever hope that these moral barriers against our race amalgamation will not stand in the way of political unity?"

When two of her own thoughtful sons can calmly write such testimonies, it is very clear that India has yet a long way to go before she is a nation.

II.

Yet NATIONALISM is a very real element in the atmosphere of India to-day, and is at its strongest and purest in many who regretfully admit that as yet India is not a nation. Here let me quote a very striking outburst of the highest nationalism from the writer of the first of the two former quotations. He is speaking to the young men of India :—

> "Be citizens of India first, and then all things else. Let your paramount pride be the pride of nationality. You have not only to maintain the traditions of old, but also to create and fashion new standards of unity, new standards of service, a new thought, new literature, new ideals. Remember always that you are the descendants of a great race, and that you have to fulfil the ultimate destiny of that race. I call it a race, because henceforth there shall be to you no castes and tongues, but one single race-people of India—the Indian race.
>
> "Remember that if Greece had her Athens, India had her Hastinapur; if Egypt had her Thebes, India had her Kanouj; if Assyria had her Babylon, India had her Ayodia; if Persia had her Persepolis, India her Kasi; if Cæsar had his Rome, Akbar had his Delhi; if Marcus Aurelius was a philosopher in ermine and linen, Asoka was a saint amid a barbaric spread of pearl and gold; if Homer gave immortality to the gods, so also Vasishta; if Cæsar wrote his 'Commentaries,' so did Baber; if Rameses built a pyramid of block granite, Shah Jehan built a dream-pyramid of white-veined marble; if heroes revelled in feats of courage and skill before the walls of Troy, we can find a nobler echo in the din of conflict upon the field of Kurekshetra. And above all, what neither Greece nor Rome nor Egypt nor Assyria nor Britain nor Gaul nor China could do,

> we did—rather our forefathers did. While Egypt gave her mysteries to the few, and Greece her mythologies to the many, Rome her philosophies to the select, Krishna gave his 'Bhagavad Gita' and Gautama his 'Dhammapada' to the million!
>
> "What son of India is there who will not glory in this country? What son of Bharata is there who will not offer a sacrifice of duty and service upon the altars of such a country?"

It is a magnificent appeal, and reveals a magnificent patriotism. To criticise some of the parallels would be an easy but an ungrateful task. Rather let us welcome an utterance that shows from what lofty sources the Nationalism of some Indians draws its inspiration. And the seer, whose impassioned words these are, is so wise in his outlook that one further quotation is justified:—

> "India in the fulness of time cannot but have complete independence. When the exact time will be, our children or their children should decide, not we. . . . We ought to prepare the way, not fix a time-limit. If India is ever to separate (from Britain) it should be a peaceful separation. . . . This may be thirty years hence, or three hundred years hence. . . . We must bear in mind the fact that not until we acquire a strong national character and national material strength can we safely dispense with the superintendence of Great Britain. The 'satanic' rule of Mr Gandhi is really an angelic rule. It gives us just the opportunity and tranquillity needed to weed out our weaknesses and manure our virtues. We learnt to think for ourselves under the safety-assuring banner of England: let us under the same banner learn to put our thoughts and our ideals in the concrete mould of achievement."

O si sic omnes! This is Indian Nationalism at its best. The more there is of this kind the better for India, for Britain, and for the world. The misfortune is that it is Nationalism of another kind altogether of which we hear most, and India hears most too: a nationalism without perspective when it surveys the past, and with a strange blindness to defects when it comes to estimate the capacities of the India of the present. But that the sounder saner nationalism is in India all the time is never to be forgotten. It has its exponents in the new National and Provincial Legislative Councils, though the other kind are there too. In our own Mother of Parliaments dare we say that all are wise? In the multiplication of the wiser exponents and the diminishing of the unwise lies India's hope.

Yet nothing is more certain than that if to-morrow the sustaining and restraining power of Britain were to be withdrawn, the day after to-morrow would see the summary end of all these Councils and the extinction of the dawning hope of an Indian nation. As things are to-day in India, the old forces that kept the peoples of India apart through all her history, are still infinitely stronger than are the forces which are slowly working for consolidation and union.

III.

There is one institution in India to-day which draws its representatives from all parts and all races of India, which holds its great Assemblies and Councils, and which would continue to hold them, even if Britain's connection with India ended, and India were broken into fragments once again. *This is the Christian Church.* India does not contain another institution so truly national. It is *Indian* to a degree that the Councils of the State know nothing of. It knows no distinctions of race or colour or station. It is not of Bengal nor Madras nor Bombay nor the Panjab: it is of India. The antagonisms of Hindu and Mohammedan are here unknown, the separating influences between caste man and out-caste do not exist. All are Indian, and Indian they will remain, whatever may come. The Church is Indian; its members are brothers one of another, and through the Church they have realised, first of all India's people, what an Indian nation means.

To-day the very intensity of this realisation is the cause of difficulties in the work of Christian Missions. Some instances of this have been referred to in the narrative of our Pilgrimage, and many more might be given. The spirit of Nationalism, which is active and vocal in Indian politics, is active and vocal in Church matters too. It would be strange were it otherwise; and here too it finds exponents, wise and unwise. In the Church, as in the State, there are extremists and there are moderates, ardent leaders who think that the time has come when the Church will best progress by living her own life, quite apart from the Mother Churches of the West, to whom she owes her birth. And there are other leaders who more truly represent the mind of the rank and file of the membership, when they urge that the time for such separation has not yet come. Leaders of the former section sometimes are apt to say things in their keen enthusiasm that jar upon the ear of the Mother Churches, who have not ceased to love their Indian children, though admittedly they have been slow to realise how very much these children of theirs have grown. But then the words of the moderate men are heard, and the note of affection that was obscured in the former speech here gets emphasised. It seemed to me when in India that the extremer spokesmen for the Indian Church were rather given to taking their cue from the politicians of the same class, and were too forgetful of the essential difference existing between the relationship borne to the Indian Church by the Churches of Britain, and that which Britain bears to India. Britain, in the Providence of God, has been and is the guardian of India; but the tie that links the Churches of these two countries together is of a much more tender and intimate kind. The Churches of the

West have been the mothers and the nursing-mothers of the Church now rising into prominence in India. There is a family tie here too sacred to be lightly severed.

Just at present, where the national note in Church life is heard most strongly is in the desire expressed by many Indian Christian leaders for a larger share in the guidance and the management of the Missions sent from the Western Churches. It is an echo, or a parallel, of the political developments in the State. There the system of a Diarchy is being tried: certain departments of the public service being entrusted to Indian Ministers of State, who are responsible to the Indian Legislature, while other departments are 'reserved' for the control of the Imperial Government. Something of the same kind is what is now urged for adoption by the Missions—a Diarchy under which parts of the Mission operations would be 'transferred' to the Indian Church Councils or Presbyteries, and other parts 'reserved' for the control of the missionaries and the Home Boards. Of the general principle there is widespread approval; but manifestly there are circumstances in the Mission sphere that do not make the parallel of the State procedure entirely applicable. Especially is this the case in regard to the funds to be employed. The State funds 'transferred' to the administration of the Indian Legislatures are raised in India, and contributed by the people of India. The funds of the Missions are almost wholly contributed by the Churches in Britain and America—for India undoubtedly; and therefore it is right and helpful to take counsel with the Indian Church as to their best expenditure. But their source is in the West, and it would seem that, as a consequence, the preponderating voice regarding their application must still for a time be the voice of the West—or if of the East, it should have the West's approval.

These and other considerations of a like kind make the State precedent, while useful, as indicating a method, not suitable as a perfect example. But the principle of Diarchy is accepted and welcomed by all the Missions in regard to their work. What needs to be done now, and is being done, is to work out a scheme, or many schemes, of Diarchy in the allied sphere of Church and Mission, which shall give increasing scope for the healthy nationalism of the Church, add to the real efficiency of the Mission, and maintain the loving concord between Eastern Church and Western Mission unbroken.

IV.

That there are elements in the atmosphere of India to-day that make Christian Missions more difficult than they once were is unquestionable. But this also is unquestionable: these very elements are furnishing a noble inspiration and a splendid spur to the whole missionary enterprise in India. India is alive, India is at a crisis of her history, India is being tested as to her capacities, and given opportunities of triumphant response such as in all her long history her people never yet have had. And Christian Missions hold in their gift the one Power that can make India emerge purified, justified, and triumphant! That Power is Christ. Only in Christ will India find the unity that will at long last make her a nation. But she will find it in Him. What an appeal to the Christian Churches lies in that one fact! What a ringing call to Christian knighthood! It is no easy enterprise to which the call gives summons. Nay, it is the most difficult in the whole wide Field of Missions, and there lies its glory. India is the 'Western Front' in the Holy War. It is the front where the fight for Christ is perhaps the very hardest, and will be very long; but it is the fight where victory will mean the final triumph of the Lord.

PRINTED IN GREAT BRITAIN BY WILLIAM BLACKWOOD AND SONS.

The Pilgrims.